A DIFFERENT EXISTENCE

A DIFFERENT EXISTENCE

PRINCIPLES OF
PHENOMENOLOGICAL PSYCHOPATHOLOGY

J. H. VAN DEN BERG, PH.D., M.D.
Professor of Medical Psychology
University of Leiden

Duquesne University Press, Pittsburgh

Published by arrangement with Uitgeverij G. F. Callenbach, N.V.
Published in Dutch as De Psychiatrische Patient.

Duquesne University Press
600 Forbes Avenue
Pittsburgh, Pennsylvania 15282

Sixteenth Printing - January 1996

Library of Congress Catalog Card Number: 72-182104
International Standard Book Number: 0-8207-0244-7
(formerly 0-391-00825-0)

Contents

A Different Existence

Introduction

This concise general psychopathology is of a somewhat unusual structure. As a rule, a general psychopathology consists of a summary of symptoms and syndromes and descriptions of general diseases; a patient's case is described only to illustrate the matter under discussion. In this book, the morbid condition of a single patient is described, and the reader is offered no definition of psychiatric symptoms, or summary of syndromes, or descriptions of general diseases. The books in which this has been done, and done well, suffice. To mention two of them, there are Dr. R. Vedder's *Inleiding tot de psychiatrie* and, for those who want a more extensive work, Jaspers' unsurpassed *Algemeine Psychopathologie*. My intention is to show that a single patient, no matter to which group his illness belongs, embodies the entire psychopathology.

The patient discussed here unmistakably belongs to the group of seriously disturbed neurotics. Yet his perceptions are abnormal in the sense that they are like hallucinations, and his thinking is neurotic like that of a patient suffering from delusions. Of course, it would be incorrect to deny borderlines where they do exist. Hallucinations and neurotic perceptions differ just as delusive and neurotic thoughts do. But the differences are not such that no relationship remains or, put more

3

carefully, the differences are not so unbridgeable that when the one is comprehended more fully no understanding of the other is gained simultaneously. All patients share the same human existence. Thus, I hope, by discussing my single patient, to create understanding of other patients, in principle of all patients, although I know that my book is small and calls for modesty.

The meaning of psychopathology described on a phenomenological foundation cannot be stated in a few words. Here and there, in the following pages, I shall try to define it more clearly. A general impression, however, should clarify phenomenology. One of its main characteristics is that it does not offer a fine theory but, rather, gives a plausible insight. The reader has a right to use his own mind upon finishing this book, even if the subject is outside his own area of competence; for the reader also shares the same human existence that makes this study, if I may be permitted to say so, also concern his life.

The patient whose complaints are described here does not exist. He does not, because no patient is described whose complaints could be recognized. He does insofar as his complaints belong together, as those of one patient. I know him, my patient—I meet him in every one of my patients.

CHAPTER ONE

What Questions are Suggested by the Complaints of Almost Every Patient?

1. A PATIENT APPEARS AT THE PSYCHIATRIST'S OFFICE

A few years ago, unusually late in the evening, I was called on the telephone by a man, evidently nervous by the sound of his voice, who asked to consult me about his personal difficulties. When I suggested some time in the next afternoon, he replied that, because of a very special reason, he preferred to see me during the evening. We agreed on the next evening, and at the appointed hour I greeted my caller, a young man of about 25 years. At first he seemed undecided, but eventually he explained the reason for his visit.

Even the first moments showed that he was in great difficulties. He looked at me with a mixture of distrust and shyness, and when he shook my extended hand, I felt a soft, weak hand, the hand of a person who doesn't know a way out and, not being in control of himself, lets himself drift. Stooping uncertainly, he sat down in the chair which I had invited him to take.

He did not relax, but sat on the edge of the chair as if preparing to get up and leave. His right hand, which he had held under his unbuttoned vest when he entered, and which he had removed from there in order to greet me so unconvincingly, was immediately replaced in its original position. With his left hand, he drummed the armrest of the chair uneasily. He did not cross his legs. His behavior created the impression of a man who has been tortured for a long time.

His story confirmed this impression entirely. He said he was a student but for many months had not attended courses because he had been unable to go into the streets during the day. The one occasion on which he had compelled himself to do so had stayed in his memory as a nightmare. He had had the feeling that the houses he passed were about to fall on him. They had seemed grey and decayed. The street had been fearfully wide and empty, and the people he had met had seemed unreal and far away. Even when someone passed him closely, he had had an impression of the distance between them. He had felt immeasurably lonely and increasingly afraid. Fear had compelled him to return to his room, and he would certainly have run if he had not been seized by such palpitations that he could only go step by step.

These palpitations had been torturing him for quite a while. In the beginning, a few years before, they had been occasional and bearable; in due course, they occurred more frequently and became fiercer. Eventually, his heart beat seemed faster than normal, even in the periods between seizures. He was continually aware of his heart, and he had to keep his hand on his chest to make sure that no abnormalities occurred and, as it were, to support and restrain his heart.

These disturbances caused him least trouble in his room.

He felt at his best when he was studying and when he was not disturbed. Apart from reading matter concerned with the subject of his studies, he had not read a novel in years. He felt certain that his heart would show more irregularities if he did. For the same reason, he did not read the newspapers either. He admitted only a few friends to his room. These people talked about nothing but their science or, when they did discuss everyday matters, were full of criticism. A slashing discussion on the female sex even brought him into relatively good health. Then he could feel delighted and he could laugh and hardly noticed his heart. His opinion of love was accordingly cynical. With approval, he cited the definition of the French moralist Chamfort, that love is nothing "but the contact of two epidermi and the exchange of two pale fantasies."

Before his illness he had had occasional contacts with a girl. When she had suggested engagement, he had laughed at her. She had left him then, and, to his surprise, at that moment his heart had started to beat violently. Afterward, he had made up his mind never again to establish relations with a girl. After this incident he visited prostitutes regularly, though not very often. He humiliated these women in every way but never actually touched them.

Once every three months he spent the weekend with his parents; they lived about 12 miles from where he lived. He always took the late train, and during the voyage, he usually felt miserable. As soon as he arrived home, he felt a delicious restfulness in his body, but this pleasant feeling disappeared in a few hours because he was increasingly irritated by his parents' behavior. He considered his father badly mannered and boorish. And when his mother sat beside him and sympa-

7

thetically inquired after his studies, heat flamed high inside him and he had to restrain himself not to slap her face. In this house, where every corner and every piece of furniture reminded him of his childhood, recollections of the past made him want to tax his parents with his misery in the meanest terms. He was always happy to leave again. In the train he was usually able to find himself an empty compartment, where, in a cold voice, he could abuse his parents. Back in his rooms, he dispelled the thoughts of his past by burying himself in a book.

He did not, or did not want to, think of the future. Life, to him, was just to study, without any purpose. If, now and then, circumstances compelled him to think of things to come, everything became vague and frightening.

So far, this is the patient's story at his first visit.

2. THE PATIENT'S COMPLAINTS

For a better understanding, the summary of the patient's complaints related at his first visit will be completed with particulars he added during later visits. For clarity, I shall categorize the complaints. Restricting myself to the patient's own information, I can classify his complaints in four groups: the changes that took place in the observable world, the changes in his body, the changes in the way he related to other people, and the changes that occurred in his past and his view of his future. So that I do not give these changes a premature interpretation, I shall keep to the classification suggested by the complaints themselves.

a) *The world*

The change in the observable world is such that the patient does not dare to leave the house during the daytime. When I ask the patient to describe what he saw, he says that the street seemed very wide and that the houses appeared colorless, gray and so old and dilapidated that they seemed about to collapse.

The houses also gave an impression of being closed up, as if all the windows were shuttered, although he could see this was not so. He had an impression of closed citadels. And, looking up, he saw the houses leaning over toward the street, so that the strip of sky between the roofs was narrower than the street on which he walked. On the square, he was struck by an expanse that far exceeded the width of the square. He knew for certain that he would not be able to cross it. An attempt to do so would, he felt, end in so extensive a realization of emptiness, width, rareness and abandonment that his legs would fail him. He would collapse.

From the security of his room, the street outside looked less ominous. Yet even there, he could not imagine himself walking or standing in the street without getting the same impressions. Aside from visiting his parents, he had not been outside the city, in the open country, or in the woods, for years. Yet he knew what would happen if he should go there. His parents lived in the country; from their house, he could see the fields. His bedroom window even gave him a wide and really magnificent view. Or rather, he remembered finding it magnificent in the past; but he had long since ceased to appreciate it. The color of the flowering fields and trees made no impression upon him; everything seemed lifeless and without color. But it was the expanse, above all, that frightened him. So, in the country, too, he could not take even the shortest walk. He used to take a taxi when he had to go to the railway station.

The patient's description of all this was so convincing that one wondered whether he lived in another world—a world just as real as the ordinary, sound world. The impression that the patient was talking about something that was real to him became even stronger when one realized how much he suffered as a result of his observations. There were no questions of fantasy or delusion. A reality defined his actions. It was simply impossible for him to deny his frightening experiences in the street; he did see things that way. The objects of his world were frightening and ominous, and when he tried to establish that the house, the street, the square and the fields would reasonably have retained their former shape and nature, and that, therefore, his perceptions must have provided him with a falsification of reality, this correction, in which he wanted to believe, if only for a moment, seemed unreal and artificial to him. It was more unreal than the direct, incorrect observation which was so frightening that it drove him back to his room. What he perceived was a reality, just as he described it.

Let us assume that I am accompanying the patient on a walk. It is a clear day; the sun is shining; people are out in the street, which does not look at all unfriendly. We can see this from the patient's window. He confirms my observations, although he perceives danger. We go outside. There the change sets in. Just outside the door, the patient grabs my arm, his face gets a glassy expression and he looks about anxiously. When I ask what the trouble is, he replies that the street frightens him. It looks so strange. So wide, and yet so narrow. The houses lean over the street, he expects them to collapse. I talk to him quietly and tell him that there is nothing wrong with the street, that it even looks quite agreeable, but he shakes his head and is not convinced. No, the further we go— in spite of my quieting words, so much based on reality—the more anxious he becomes. He clutches my arm as if he feels that he is not given enough support. Sweat is on his forehead. He looks as if something serious is about to happen. He wants to return home, for God's sake! There he wipes the sweat from his face and smiles wearily. A normal person would be inclined to ask: what had happened. There was nothing wrong with the street; it should have had no effect on the patient. He doesn't see it that way. He might even say, "You have no idea of what happened out there."

It is a good thing to remember this: that which, in the street, seems real to the patient, does not exist in our view. So the patient must be deluding himself. How he deludes himself, however, is not clear. Even that he deludes himself remains obscure.

b) *The body*

The physical complaints of the patient, who doesn't seem to be physically ill, mainly concern his heart. I have already mentioned the fits of palpitations. Initially these seizures were bearable, but gradually they became so violent that he was afraid he was going to collapse from weakness. In between seizures he has a pain in his chest. There is something wrong in his chest; something is going to break down. He is afraid that his heart is going to stop. That is why he keeps his hand under his vest; he wants to be present when his heart gives out. His pulse has a too fast and slightly irregular rhythm. Perhaps the patient should consult a cardiologist. He tells us, however, that he has consulted a number of cardiologists, who have all assured him that there was nothing wrong with his heart. He hands over a letter from the last cardiologist he consulted, the one who has advised him to see a psychiatrist. From this letter it appears that an extensive examination had revealed no defects apart from the too fast heartbeat and a slightly irregular pulse.

The patient is still not convinced that his heart is all right. In his opinion, if finer methods of examination were used, defects would certainly be found. Does he not have evidence of the correctness of his opinion? A few steps in the street show how his heart behaves. If he should go on, he knows that his heart will stop beating. And besides, does his heart not hurt all day long? Letters from all the cardiologists in the world could not make him accept the fact that the pain he feels does not exist and that there is nothing wrong with his heart. His heart is ill; that is the reality of his physical life.

Apart from this, the patient complains of weakness in his legs and a disturbed sense of equilibrium. Almost every evening, when it is dark and the streets look less alarming, he takes a walk. At first, this caused him no trouble, but later he could not walk without the support of a strong stick. Later still, even the stick became inadequate, and he could walk only if he walked beside his bicycle, holding the handlebars with both hands. Since then he has never gone out without his bicycle. His neighbors, who think that he goes out for a ride in the evening are wrong. He couldn't even sit on the bicycle; the mere thought makes him dizzy. When sidewalks are slippery in the winter, he stays home. He is very particular about the shoes he buys; he cannot afford running the risk of slipping and losing his balance.

It is hardly necessary to state that the patient had consulted an otologist. He had been examined and had been told that there was nothing wrong with his sense of equilibrium. He was not to worry about that. Yet the patient had continued to worry and had consulted a neurologist, who had also told him that there were no defects.

All this leads to the same conclusion: objective and conscientious examinations indicate no physiological bases for the symptoms that are causing the patient so much trouble. He must be deluding himself without being aware of it. For who can doubt the result of a modern, medical, objective, scientific examination?

c) The other people

When the patient is asked to express his opinion about other people, one thing becomes obvious: he has no real contact with anyone. Everyone irritates him. When his parents talk about everyday matters, he finds them credulous, too optimistic and too romantic. He objects to the word "friend," for friendship, according to him, is camouflaged egotism. He calls the fellow students who come and talk to him about his science acquaintances, not friends. They are useful where his studies are concerned, but that is the only reason he can bear them. And the people who discuss, in a disparaging way, subjects concerning the values of life, certainly give him monents of pleasure, but he would not like to call him friends either. He is quite undecided where girls are concerned. He prefers to have nothing to do with them. In his opinion, they are inferior creatures who are mainly concerned with matters that are frightening to him. In his eyes, his relationships with prostitutes are the only kinds of relationship a man can have with a woman. Love is all nonsense—although he admits that this nonsense does not leave him alone. For this reason, he does not read novels. To retain his tranquility, he has to avoid any-

13

thing that might remind him of normal human relationships. That is why he does not read a newspaper.

The people in the street remain at a curious distance, which gives him a feeling of abandonment. Even when they touch him, on the sidewalk, he still feels the distance. They move senselessly, in a street that is too wide, like lifeless puppets. They make him feel lonely, restless, anxious and angry. He would like to destroy these puppets. All human beings are his enemies.

Common sense tells us that the patient must be wrong again. He is the victim of a misunderstanding of his own making. For, if it is true from a sound point of view that society is controlled by ambition and self-interest, just as obvious is the evidence of true friendship and love. But this evidence is positively denied by the patient. He can enumerate many incidents illustrating that friendship is no more than pretense. Discussing the subject with him has no effect. That which is quite obvious to anyone else does not exist in his view. The patient lives in another reality, also, in his relations with other people. He clearly illustrates this other reality when he describes what people look like. To him, they are as puppets controlled by evil. He wants to have nothing to do with them. He wants nothing from them. He would not be able, for that matter, to get anything from them, for they are too far away. He cannot reach anyone, and no one can reach him. Even when people are touching him they remain at a distance in the most literal sense of the word. Is this not a contradiction? It is no contradiction to the patient. One could argue with him with all the persuasiveness at one's disposal that when people are touching one another, there can be no perception of distance between them; but it would not do any good. He perceives distance and he

14

feels it, so what is the use of arguing? Something that is unnoticed by anyone, and, when suggested, is denied by everyone, appears to be a reality to the patient.

d) *Past and future*

It is striking with how much aversion the patient speaks of his past. He says he remembers little from his childhood; but the few things he does remember give him a right, he thinks, to conclude that he has had a bad upbringing. He says his father always kept him short, his mother spoiled him and neither of them prepared him for the hard life before him. As a rule, he does not think much about these things. But when he goes home to see his parents, incidents from his past come to his mind. In every room of his parental home he is aware of his childhood. He feels that his parents are still treating him like a child; they are still making the same mistakes they made in the past. He is certain that his father's feelings toward him are hostile. His monthly allowance—he must always ask for it—is inadequate. Every inquiry from his father about his studies is an act of distrust. When his father asks him how he feels, he perceives a tone of reproach and malicious delight. He gets angry, then, and would prefer to leave and never come back, if it were not for the fact that he knows himself to be financially dependent. His mother may have his best interest at heart, but he still has to resist her, for if he should react to her questions, he would feel himself small and would probably cry. This would be unbearable and would undermine his whole attitude toward life. So he must resist her. Only when he is cold and businesslike does life remain bearable. That is why his replies to his mother's questions are chilling statements. And when she persists, he leaves the room.

A considerable time after the treatment had been concluded,

15

I received information from two different sources about the family conditions, of which the patient gave so gloomy an account. One was a colleague of the patient who knew the parents well, and the other was an acquaintance who had often visited the family when the patient had been a child. Their stories coincided in that they provided me with a completely different picture of the parents. The father, I gathered, was a reticent man who was absorbed in his work but who never put his family completely out of his mind. He was strict with his children, but not hard or unfeeling. He had permitted them to choose their own profession and had never stinted them in the means to live. The mother was described by both as a gentle woman, inclined to be sentimental, who had made life too easy for her children, but not to such an extent as the patient had indicated. To outsiders, they had seemed quite a normal family.

The other children had maintained normal relations with their parents. As a child, the patient had not been very noticeable. He had not given more trouble than his brothers and sisters. He had always been quite happily engaged in his games, but they were mostly solitary games. When there was a party, he had amused the family with his jokes. His imitation of the village teacher had been very popular; when he was doing his imitation, he had seemed a born teacher. At times, his words had been malicious, but he was only a child, so no one had taken them amiss. Only when he was growing up did his parents become aware that he did not feel happy at home. At first, they took these signs as puberty symptoms, and they gave him more freedom. But he did not react the way they expected. They were glad that he wanted to study, because they had hoped that the freedom of student life would solve the difficulties, of whose nature they were unaware. Anxiously, they had noticed his condition getting worse.

Again, the difference between the patient's story and the statements of objective onlookers must be emphasized. One is inclined to choose the reports of the witnesses. Is the satisfactory development of the other children of the family indication that the patient must have been wrong? It could be considered evidence. Yet nothing would be gained by confronting the patient with this argument. To try to convince him is of no use; he will not be convinced, and he will be inclined to complain about so much misunderstanding. Arguing with him could even result in a disaster. Every psychiatrist knows that, if therapy is to have any effect, there is no sense in discussing a thing like this with the patient. This is also true for all the other inconsistencies. Speaking from a psychotherapeutic point of view, one would be incorrect in telling the patient that he is deluding himself in his observation of the street, that he is mistaken in his opinion about the condition of his heart and that he has a deceptive impression of people around him. I shall return to this later. The point to make here is to conclude that the patient differs from others in recalling the past and that he takes his different opinion for the reality of his childhood.

A similar situation obtains with respect to the future. If the patient—we would like to argue—would almost shout at him —he would only open his eyes and see what the world is really like, see how healthy his body is in reality, see how good the intentions of the people around him are in reality, see how well he has been brought up, actually. If he only saw these

17

things, he would be able to expect everything from the future. He is young, intelligent, of good stock and not without means. He has a pleasant face (if he did not look so gloomy and angry) and he has charming manners. The future is open to him. But when he is asked about it, he has nothing to say about the future. He does not know what is going to happen to him and he fears the worst. All the expectations, so good, so true, are drowned in his lamentation that the future does nothing but leer at him.

3. ANALYSIS OF THE PROBLEM

In the foregoing section, the patient's complaints were classified under four headings. In every instance, a contradiction existed between the patient's opinion and the facts of reality. Even if it is true that not every psychiatric patient draws attention to all four of these contradictions, it is not often that, listening to the story of a person who is mentally ill, one does not hear at least part (usually a considerable part) of the summary. I have pointed out that it is of no use to confront the patient with these contradictions; this is common knowledge among psychiatrists and psychotherapists. Besides, the patient is sick and tired of this kind of discussion. He has heard so often from relatives, friends and acquaintances that his opinions are wrong. These discussions never did him any good; they irritated him and made him feel bad. He visits the psychotherapist in order to hear another answer. And he gets another answer. The following is the usual train of thought of the psychotherapist.

a) Projections

When the patient says that the houses seem gray and decayed and lean over dangerously and that the fields show little life or color, in other words, that the world looks different during the moments that he is frightened, the psychotherapist is not in the least inclined to believe—with the patient—that the things, the objects themselves, have changed. He still considers his own observations correct and those of the patient incorrect. The patient must be mistaken; in this, he agrees with the patient's relatives, friends and acquaintances. But the psychotherapist does not say so. He does not tell the patient he is wrong. For one thing, because he knows that his patient cannot be convinced by such a statement. And for another, because he knows that such a statement would not help the patient to get better. But, above all, because, in a way, he agrees with the patient. Something has changed indeed; in this, the patient is not mistaken. But the outside world has not changed. The patient himself, his subject, has become mentally ill, which means that he has changed. The patient is mistaken in the location of the change. The psychotherapist believes that the patient has shifted his defective state of mind toward the objects he perceives. To put it in technical words: the patient projects. He projects onto the things around him that which, after all, really exist within his own self.

We have become familiar with the concept of projection. So much so that we are hardly, if at all, aware of the theoretical difficulties this concept implies. And yet, no one has ever been able to explain the way a projection takes place. One must realize that there is no acceptable theory to explain how an abnormal mood, a mental disturbance, that is, something within the patient, could leave him, move toward objects of the outside world, and attach themselves to these objects, merge into them, so that the patient perceives them as a reality, simultaneously losing the memory of actual reality. But one

19

thing is certain: the world about which the patient speaks is as real to him as our world is to us. His world is even more real than ours; for, whereas we are able to rid ourselves of the spell of a depressing landscape, the patient is unable to liberate himself from his gloomy scenery. This patient even stayed at home to avoid being disturbed by the objects he would see in the street. Could this fact be in accordance with the concept of projection? As soon as we realize what projection means, we are faced with an enigma.

b) Conversion

Then the physical complaints. About these, too, the psychotherapist agrees with the relatives' and friends' point of view. He thinks, too, that the patient's body is quite healthy. Even if at first, because of the patient's suffering appearance, he may have had his doubts, his doubts have been removed by the communications of other specialists. Still, the psychotherapist does not assume that the patient is pretending or that he is suffering from an imaginary illness. The patient is really ill; the therapist does not doubt that. But his illness is unlike the one he thinks he has; it is not a physical, but a mental illness. He is putting his mental illness in the place of his body's organs. The psychiatrist calls this change "conversion."

The term "conversion," also, has been generally adopted in psychiatry. Obviously, the concept of conversion is just as obscure as the concept of projection. Let us see what the word implies. The reasoning is as follows. A human being consists of two parts, a body and a soul. The parts are unalike. In contrast with the soul, the body is visible and dissectable; it is an object. The soul, according to the general opinion, is contained

20

within this object—where exactly is difficult to say. Every effort to discover the location of the soul has failed. Still, several organs are necessary for the existence of a mental life. The heart is one of these organs. The brain, we are even less able to do without. And of the brain, the midbrain is particularly associated with the existence of that which has been designated as soul. Still enigmatic is where the connection is effected. Dissecting these organs, one never finds thoughts, desires or memories; never fear, hope, love or hate. Nothing that could be called soul can be found within the body. But this does not surprise us; did we not start from the assumption that the soul is invisible and undissectable? Then it does not occupy space. But one would be incorrect in assuming that the soul is located within the body. That which does not occupy space cannot be inside or outside anything. The assumption that man has a body and soul and that this soul, which does not take up space, is contained within a three-dimensional body is obscure. The statement that mental difficulties expresses themselves physically is a transgression of a metaphysical gap. No one knows what this statement means.

Still, supposing that something like a spaceless soul does exist within the body, how are we to conceive of this soul, which contains neither space nor matter, to affecting the body? Thinkers like Descartes and Leibniz thought about this in vain. There is no basis for the assumption that a nonphysical thing, called soul, physically affects the organs of a body. The assumption is even a contradiction, an intrinsic impossibility. This conclusion was reached by Leibniz, who, consequently, formulated the theory that ever since creation, body and soul go their separate ways, as two divided systems, closed within themselves—ways for which the Creator, at the beginning of time, had set a course so perfectly parallel that we, deceived by appearances, decided that there was a continuous contact. With every act, the decision would not lead to the deed, but decision and deed would each result, independently, from independent sequences of events, starting from creation—a sequence of events of the body and a sequence of events of the soul. No one still credits this theory. Nor could anyone still believe, with Descartes, that the pineal gland, situated in the center of the brain, is the, one could say occult, spot where body and soul are linked.

Does the psychiatrist have to puzzle his head over these philosophical problems? The question is not correct. The psychiatrist who speaks of conversion is a philosopher already, so there is no reason why one should not wonder about his philosophy. We should realize that one cannot speak of conversion without having taken for granted that, apart from the body, there is a soul and that this soul, situated within the body, maintains contact with this body. Not accepting this philosophy must result in finding another interpretation of the fact that a mentally disturbed person complains about his body. The next chapter will be dedicated to another philosophy and to the interpretation of physical complaints based on it.

But first, another comment on the irrationality of the statement that the patient converts. If it is a fact that the disturbances leading to the patient's physical complaints are of a mental rather than a physical origin, what makes the patient stress his physical complaints? More plausible for him would be to stress his mental troubles and afterward relate the effects on his body. But what we do hear from the patient is only about physical troubles—palpitations, tenseness in his stomach, a band around his head, weakness in his legs, weariness in his arms.

Occasionally, he does mention complaints that could be called mental: he feels nervous, anxious and irritated. But he measures his nervousness by the agitated feelings in his breast, by the pressure on his throat and by the shaking of his fingers, his hands and his whole body. He locates his anxiety in the region of his heart. His general displeasure is a bad taste in his mouth and a loathing in his throat. We are almost inclined to think that conversion exists the other way round: that the physical complaints are real and the mental are derivative complaints. The physical complaints do not give the impression of being converted complaints. In the patient's story, they are the most real.

c) Transference

I leave this theme now to see what line of thought is followed by the psychotherapist when he hears what the patient thinks of other people. Let me first repeat that the psychotherapist, with the patient's relatives, is not, as a rule, inclined to believe what the patient says. It cannot be true that nearly everybody means to harm him. The patient has a wrong idea about people. He must be mistaken. He errs when he thinks that all men encroach upon his personal liberty and all women are worthless creatures upsetting him with their physical attractions. How did the patient get trapped in such a misunderstanding? To this question, the psychotherapist has a decisive answer. He says that, in reality, the patient's difficulties only concern his parents. In his childhood, something went wrong. His upbringing had been no real upbringing; rather, it was an obstruction to his maturation. The patient's relations with his father became strained; he has been fighting his father ever since and is still doing so, with the peculiarity that he has shifted the scene of his battle to his contacts with other men. As for his mother, in his childhood, the patient had to defend himself against her indulging, too-binding influence. He did not succeed. He became no freer from his mother than he did from his father. He has given up the fight against his mother, also, but in vain, for no one can leave behind anything so unfinished. He has to continue the fight, and he is doing so. But instead of fighting himself free from his mother, he fights all women he meets. He conveys the emotions meant for his mother to other women. He has become the victim of transference.

This is a third term that has become a platitude in psychiatry: *transference*, the conveyance of feelings—and the contact difficulties that go with them—from one person to another, the former being the person with whom the patient is really in trouble, while the latter has nothing to do with these difficulties.

The psychotherapist witnesses impressive examples of this transference. Does he, himself, not often become the person to whom the patient transfers his emotions? Sooner or later, the patient under treatment entertains feelings toward him that only apply to other people. The psychotherapist is hated, without having given cause for hatred. He is loved, while there is no objective motive for love. Generally, the treatment explains the reason why the patient behaves like this. In his hatred, for example, he shows characteristics of his earlier contact with his father, his mother, his brother, or his sister. His love is a copy of the love gone wrong that he fostered for one of the persons of his childhood. That which was left unfinished earlier is continued in the therapist's office. The psychotherapist is not worried about this. He knows that this is the way in which the patient finds his cure. He permits the transference, if it is not in concrete form; that is, it never grows into a hand-to-hand fight or into an embrace. But apart from this, anything is permitted. The therapist offers the patient the opportunity to express his effects of earlier periods and to rid himself of the misunderstandings in which he had been caught. The patient's affective history, which could not be terminated in earlier periods, is brought to a conclusion in the therapist's office. The treatment of the patient appears to consist of the treatment of the transference. So the psychotherapist can never doubt the fact of transference. The patient recovers: is this not evidence for the correctness of his opinion?

Irrespective of this evidence, the question is justified as to the soundness of the theoretical arguments which form the underlying principle of the concept of transference. For even a concept that proves satisfactory in practice can be based on an error. To test the theory, I shall proceed from the following example.

During his childhood, a patient has grown to hate his mother because she never let him free in any way. Now he hates all women. This is the adopted train of thought: the patient transfers his hatred from the mother to other women. This construction presupposes that an effect, in this case hatred, can be disconnected from its object. So there must be something like "hatred without an object." Yet no one has ever experienced anything like an objectless hatred. No one can claim having hated without having directed his hatred against something or someone. Even "blind hatred" is directed —blindly—at something or at everything. Nondirected love is equally unknown. This observation, however, abolishes the described, apparently simple, interpretation of transference. Without a doubt, there must be something like transference; the evidence is too convincing to be denied. But the "mechanism" suggested by the word cannot be correct. Anyone who has doubts about this does well to put himself in the place of a person suffering from transference. Hating his mother, one feels his hatred as impregnated with his mother. He cannot separate his hatred from this mother, the object of this hatred. Both are one.

How did this incorrect train of thought come into existence? The cause can be found in the fact that it became the custom to treat mental qualities as if they were objects. Saying that an affect is transferred from one person to another is like observing an ashtray being moved from the table to the desk. This is all right where things are concerned. Affects are not things, however. They cannot be lifted from one place and put down at another. Here the words "lifted" and "put down" have no meaning. Just as meaningless is the word "transference"; the concept of this word belongs to physical science. If it is to make sense in psychology—and extensive experience argues in its favor—it must be psychologically defined. Until recently, such a definition has been lacking.

d) Mythicizing

Projection, conversion, transference. There is a fourth word which, by his story, the patient evokes in the psychiatrist's mind.

It has been stated that every psychotherapist is invited to

find the origin of his patient's affects in his childhood. Let us see how the patient accounts for his childhood, and let us try to find the theoretical difficulties with which we are confronted by the patient's story.

Many neurotic patients have little to say in favor of their childhoods. Often their educators appear to have been people who did not know their business. The patients mention sad circumstances: their fathers beat them often and cruelly, their mothers were either heartless or suffered from blind love. Occasionally a criminal event is reported. A father threatened to throw his son out of the house or (but this is an old story) to cut off his penis if he should persist in playing with it.

In the early years of psychotherapy, before 1900, these accounts were readily believed. They were called mental injuries, psychotraumata, and were considered the origin of the entire neurosis. Later, when it became clear that these accounts were not based on the truth, the doctrine of psychotraumata suffered discredit. Yet the neurosis had to have a cause. In the confusion of the moment, some psychiatrists shifted the psychotraumata to earlier periods—to the moment of birth, for example, or even to prehistoric ages of mankind. Boys would have been emasculated and fathers eaten. If, at first, this theory seemed to be confirmed by the study of (then called) primitive races, a closer acquaintance with these races made the investigator very cautious. The ethnologists appeared least eager to accept this supposition. Since then, this hypothesis, too, has been abandoned, and a great many other theories have been formulated to explain the origin of neuroses. It remained difficult, however, to understand why the patient gives an account of his past, contradictory to the actual course of events.

Also in this matter, the psychotherapist agrees in principle

27

with the relatives and acquaintances: the patient must be mistaken. If not, it would, first of all, be difficult to explain how, in the same family, other children could mature without neuroses. As for our patient, moreover, reliable statements from two sources prevent us from believing that the parents were the sort of people the patient described. But here, too, the therapist does not merely say that the patient is mistaken. Following the French psychiatrist Dupré, he will observe that the patient, as a result of his neurosis, is the victim of a mythicizing of his past.[1] The patient suffers from memory falsifications. His memory is making a myth, a legend, out of his past.

Is the psychiatrist aware that he is denying, with these words, the current conception of memory, a conception he probably accepts himself? To remember, according to this conception, is to make conscious the *engrammata* recorded in the brain. If something happens to a person, if a person observes something, a picture of what was observed (according to this conception) attaches itself to the brain. As a rule, this is represented as a purely physiological process. With perception, the lens of the eye throws a more or less accurate picture of the perceived scene on the retina; by way of certain nerves, this picture is conveyed, also more or less accurately, to centers in the brain, where it anchors. To remember means: back to this anchorage. Of course, disturbances can occur in this process. For example, the memory may not mark out the original anchorage accurately; the memory then becomes contaminated with associations to other memories, and so on. In such a case we usually suspect that a disturbance has occurred. We

1. E. Dupré, *Pathologie de l'imagination et de l'emotivite.* Paris, 1925. Dupré speaks of activite and of mythomanie; neither term seems very applicable in the Dutch text. Thus, the word: mythicizing.

28

say that we cannot hit upon it, that we cannot recollect it or that our memory fails us. Saying this, we expect a correction as soon as things "come back to us clearly," which happens most quickly when someone who was with us at the time of the perception or experience "reminds us."

Nothing of the kind is observed in the patient. If we make efforts, armed, if desired, with the account of eyewitnesses, to cure him from his errors, he holds on energetically to what we call his mistakes. How could such behavior be explained by the theory of the *engrammata*? What is the sense, here, to speak of falsification, of mythicizing? Can engrammata be overlaid by a myth? Supposing that this is possible, how then can one explain that the patient believes his myth to be the truth and the truth to be an error? Why does he not have a suspicion of his mistakes? If we could only accept that the patient is deceiving us!

e) The unconscious

But we abandon this consideration when we talk to him. The patient behaves in good faith. Here, almost every psychotherapist gives me his support by stating that the deceit committed by the patient is present indeed, but remains unconscious. The same observation must, in all honesty, be made about all the discussed contradictions. The patient projects his subjective condition onto the things of his daily existence, but he projects unconsciously. The patient has physical disturbances that cannot be confirmed by any medical examination; he converts, but he converts unconsciously. The patient believes the people around him hostile; he is the victim of transference, but he transfers unconsciously. He overlays his memory with a myth, but he mythicizes unconsciously.

With this, once more everything is acceptable. No effort is

needed to maintain the criticized concepts of projection, conversion, transference and mythicizing if, in addition, the unconscious is accepted. The method is simple. With every theoretical difficulty, a quality that solves this difficulty is attributed to the unconscious. When, for instance, it is established that hatred without an object does not exist, so that transference of hatred is an impossibility, one can presume that the unconscious is the area within which objectless emotions do occur, so that there an affect can be separated from its original object. Then a transference of an affect from one object to another is possible. The criticism of the concept of transference then becomes powerless, the more so because the means of verification are lacking. Is not the unconscious, by definition, that which escapes attention? The unconscious is not experienced; there is no sense in appealing to experience.

Yet there is one more objective. From a psychological point of view, the trains of thought accompanying projection, conversion, transference and mythicizing appeared weak or even untenable. What should we think when the train of thought is saved by an argument that leaves the province of psychology: the unconscious is not to be experienced mentally. As soon as it is experienced, it stops being unconscious. Many psychopathologists acknowledge this difficulty. They feel like physical scientists who are invited to explain unsolved physical problems with the aid of the occult.

The unconscious (in addition to many matters) is evidence of a premature solution of the theoretical difficulties presented by the psychiatric patient. Let us set aside the hypothesis of the unconscious and look into the discrepancies between the patient's story and the "facts of reality." To do this, we give attention to the following questions.

1. What is the relationship, in general, of oneself and objects, and what can be said about this relationship when there is mental disturbance?

2. What is the relationship of oneself and one's body, and what is the relationship when there is a mental disturbance?

3. What is the relationship, also in general, of oneself and other people, and what is the relationship when there is a mental disturbance?

4. What is the relationship of oneself and one's past, or, more in general, and time, and what can be said about this relationship when there is a mental disturbance? This leads to a final, important question: is it necessary to accept an unconscious mental life?

CHAPTER TWO

The Answers

1. MAN AND WORLD

It is winter. Evening is falling, and I get up to switch on the light. Looking outside, I see that it has started to snow. Everything is covered by glittering snow, falling down silently out of a heavy sky. People are moving soundlessly past my window. I hear someone stamping the snow from his feet. I rub my hands and look forward to the evening, for a few days ago I telephoned a friend to ask him if he could spend this evening with me. In an hour he will be standing before my door. The snow outside seems to make his visit even more pleasant. Yesterday, I bought a bottle of good wine, which I put at the proper distance from the fire.

I sit down at my desk to answer some mail. After a half-hour, the telephone rings. My friend is calling to say that he cannot come. We exchange a few words and make another appointment. When I put down the receiver, the stillness of my room has become slightly more pronounced. The hours to come seem longer and emptier. I put a log on the fire and return to my desk. A few moments later, I am absorbed in a book. The evening slips away slowly.

When I look up a moment to think over a passage that refuses to become clear, the bottle by the fire catches my eye.

Once more, I realize that my friend will not come, and I return to my book.

Reviewing this episode taken from everyday life, I notice that there is a continuous interaction between me, the subject, and the things around me, the objects. I am expecting my friend; this subjective condition is visible to me through the objects in my room. I light the fire, arrange cigarettes and let the wine get to the proper temperature. Even to another, my subjective condition (at this point) is quite apparent; coming in unexpectedly, one would say: "I see that you are expecting company." Then, it snows; this objective condition appears capable of adding to my subjective expectation. When the telephone puts an end to this expectation, the silence of the room is more pronounced. When, later on, I see the bottle, this objective actuality tells me that my subjective expectation is cancelled.

An interaction. Now the question as to the nature of this interaction. To find the answer, I concentrate on the last observation: I see the bottle of wine and I realize that my friend will not come. What happens at this moment? Or, more precisely: what do I see when I observe the bottle of wine? The question seems trivial and the answer is accordingly simple. I see a green bottle with a white label, on which is printed a mark.

At closer examination, I can read the printed words. It is a bottle of Médoc. The bottle is corked and sealed with a lead capsule. I could go on in this way and sum up all the details of the bottle. But it becomes obvious to me that, writing down these facts, I don't get any nearer to that which I was observing when, looking up, I saw the bottle. What I was seeing then

34

was not a green bottle, with a white label, with a lead capsule, and things like that. What I was really seeing was something like the disappointment about the fact that my friend would not come or about the loneliness of my evening. Of course, I did see a bottle with a white label, a capsule, etc., but my seeing these things meant that I jumped over the object, bottle, to the value this bottle had acquired for me this evening.

The behavioristic psychologist, with his positivism, who is adapted to the laws of physical science, will tell me now that this is pure poetry. He will explain to me that I did see a glass bottle, with a label and with a capsule, but that I furnished this observation with matters not belonging to it. I contaminated the observation with the projection of a condition, the condition of being disappointed and lonely. This raises a question: if I had been seeing my projection, and if I had asked how I felt toward myself instead of toward the bottle, would I not have observed my loneliness more distinctly, while less adulterated, with more reality, more directly? Introspection would have shown me how I felt. Well, then, it appears not to be so. As soon as I ask myself, by introspection, how I feel, instead of a more refined, I get a less distinct realization of my loneliness. Worse: if I try, by introspection, that is, by leaving out everything that is outside myself to investigate my feelings, I don't know what to do. I'm standing in front of a blind wall. Every effort, purely by myself, to summon my loneliness results in a realization of what is there: my room, the fire, the bottle and, within all this, my absent friend.

Another example. A married couple who visited Venice on their honeymoon makes a trip to the same city ten years later. In the train, they remember several incidents. Once again, the city of Venice comes to life for them. But they only realize what Venice meant to them before when they set foot in a gondola and sit down in the *felza*, when they see the palaces, when they hear the gondoliers calling and when they sniff the Adriatic water. Venice—there it is! The introspection in the train brought back some memories, certainly, but no more than shadows of the memories which come to them in the white facades, in the sounds and in the smells. Are tourists not invited to accept that memory, this extremely subjective condition anchored within the voices, the smells, within the objects, within everything there? If this is so, the psychologist is not allowed to shift the accents. Does he not try to describe the facts?

If he tries to describe the facts, he will find an error in the previous paragraph. The introspection in the train is what I wrote about. Was it really introspection? Was the couple looking into their own souls when they were talking about Venice? Or were they looking back through the period of ten years to the Venice of those days, the Venice there, of the time when they were newlyweds? Does something like introspection really exist? In other words, is there really a pure subject? I shall leave this question for the time being. The matter under discussion now is that the pure object does not exist. Of this, another example.

The fact that an object carries the same name under different circumstances does not guarantee its being the same under those different circumstances. Take an oak tree, for instance. The oak tree here and the oak tree there carry the same name. The oak tree in a wood in Normandy and the oak tree in a square in Berlin. But what a difference! No doubt this differ-

ence is traceable to the difference within the spectat
a different person in a wood in Normandy from what one is
in Berlin. But this difference exists because Normandy and
Berlin differ. The oak tree plays a part in this difference. An
oak tree without anything—without a place—does not exist.
The oak tree is different.

This last statement requires effort to be understood. Understanding is easier when we consider another example of the
same order and put the question whether the same oak tree,
in the same place, is always the same to different people. The
answer is "no."[2] To the hunter, the oak tree is a shelter for
birds and an opportunity to find cover for himself. To the
timber dealer, the oak tree is an object that can be measured,
counted and sold. To the young, romantic girl, it is part of
her love-landscape. All these persons see different oaks. And
yet they see the same oak. A contradiction? It is indeed a contradiction if we do not distinguish two forms of perception.
If perception means unemotional, scientific observations, mea-
surement and confirmation, the three people see exactly the
same thing: an oak tree, a tree, shaped in a certain way, with
trunk, branches, leaves and fruit—*Quercus robur* in botany.

But the psychologist can do little with this object and with
the perception connected with it. As a rule, ours is another
kind of perception. Never do we see objects without anything
else. Even the *Quercus robur* is more than an object. We see
things within their context and in connection with ourselves:
a unity which can be broken only to the detriment of the parts.
A sigificant unity. We might say that we see the significance

2. The example is from J. von Uexküll and G. Kriszat, *Streidzuge durch
die Umwelten von Tieren und Menschen.* Hamburg, 1956.

things have for us. If we don't see the significance, we don't see anything at all. This is, once more, also true for the botanist. If he sees no *Quercus robur*, he sees nothing as a botanist. The romantic girl sees qualities of the oak tree of which the timber dealer would not dream (unless, perhaps, when he is looking at her). In turn, the timber dealer observes characteristics that are nonexistent to the girl. Both, however, see a reality; that is what should be stressed. One day an African, who had never seen anything but the jungle and his village, was taken to London and shown part of the city. When, at the end of his tour, he gave an account of things he had noticed, he did not mention, as would be expected, the paved streets, the brick-built houses, the cars, streetcars and trains, but he said that what had surprised him most was that one man could greet so many people so emphatically. What he had seen was a policeman, who had, with much waving of his arms been controlling the traffic. For the rest, he had seen nothing. As cars, trains, streets and brick-built houses were of no significance to him, he could not see them.

Whatever we see, hear, taste and smell concerns foremost, directly and purely, ourselves. The hunter sees his intention to hunt. The timber dealer shows himself and everyone around him what he is when he sees logs in the oak tree, that is, future boards and bridges and houses to be built. The girl gives evidence of her romantic disposition when she looks upon the oak tree in her way. In this manner, the married couple found again the state of their honeymoon when they once more observed the things in Venice; and I found again my disappointment when, that evening, I saw the bottle near the fire.

If we want to gain insight into another person, his condi-

tion, nature, habits or disturbances, we should not inquire
first about his introspectively accessible, subjective account of
his observations. This account, although essentially possible,
does not as a rule, contain much information. We get an impression of a person's character, of his subjectivity, of his nature and his condition when we ask him to describe the objects which he calls his own; in other words, when we inquire
about his world. Not the world as it appears to be "on second
thought," but the world as he sees it in his direct, day-to-day
observation. A "second thought" disturbs the verity of this
reality. It has been this "second thought" that has considerably
hampered the development of psychology.

These considerations need hardly be told to present-day
psychologists and psychiatrists, for, almost routinely, investigations into subjective data preferably do not include inquiries
about the patient's inner life. One, rather, hands him a set of
prints—Rorschach, or TAT, for instance—and asks him to
describe what he sees. Then it is of small interest to the psychologist what the patient observes on second thought: a man
with trousers and vest, etc. No, he tests the original observation by asking the patient what is happening in the picture;
he tries to determine the significance the objects of the pic-
tures have for the patient. He gains knowledge of the subject
by inquiring about his objects, about the solid, real things of
the world.

All this can be summarized as follows: The relationship between man and world is so close that it is erroneous to separate
them in a psychological or psychiatric examination. If they
are separated, the patient ceases to be this particular patient
and his world ceases to be his world. Our world is not pri-

39

marily a conglomeration of objects that can be described scientifically. Our world is our home, a realization of subjectivity. If we want to understand man's existence, we must listen to the language of objects. If we are describing a subject, we must elaborate on the scene in which the subject reveals itself.

We must add an observation for those who find these words too philosophical. No one is without a philosophy. He who boasts of not having any is a victim of the philosophy hiding behind his negation. The strict separation of man and world is neither natural nor original. This separation originated from a philosophy. Descartes, with others, in writings of a philosophical nature, dug a gap between man and world, between human and nonhuman matters, between, in Descartes' words, *res cogitantes* and *res extensae*. Since then, this separation has struck root to the advantage of physical science, because physical science is powerless with regard to not completely nonhuman objects. It should be just as easy to understand that a science like psychology has been handicapped by this separation. Because of it, psychology became the science of the subject, which means, ultimately, the science of an emptiness, of a nothingness. For the subject, the pure subject, the completely unsubstantial inner man, does not exist. Anyone can establish this fact by examining whether purely subjective events ever happen to him. Thinking, one thinks something, a matter ultimately always located there, yonder, outside; an object, or something concerned with objects. Feeling, one feels sympathy toward matters or people, there; one feels absence, a lack of something, an absence of something there, outside one's own self. Even the most individual and abstract imagination portrays something there, yonder: a fantasy, a dream castle, a utopia, a realm of the blessed; matters indeed not discernible by touch of hand, yet still imagined between, beside or above other matters that can be touched. Nothing belongs to us that is not bound yonder.

This makes a psychology of the strictly subjective meaningless. There is no such psychology. This has been realized by many psychologists, who consequently, however, convinced that Descartes' separation was unassailable, swerved to physiology. Out of impotence, the psychologists became physiologist, or (what comes to the same thing) behaviorist, surveyor, arithmetician. The psychologist stopped believing in mental qualities. Yet the psychologist has to believe in these qualities if he desires to remain psychologist. Very well, he can believe in them. As soon as he does away with Descartes' separation, which is not valid in everyday life, he is psychologist again. Yet this is only possible in a philosophical argument that invalidates Descartes' argument. Here is another example explaining the Cartesian point of view and the necessity of philosophical reflection upon it.

"Libido" is a word often encountered in psychological and psychiatric publications. The underlying reasoning is as follows. The body consists of liquids and cells, the latter often combined into groups, glands. Glands have ducts through which the liquid produced by the cells flows to another place. The endocrine glands, however, have no draining ducts and they empty their liquid, called hormones, directly into the blood. Among these, the sexual glands are of particular significance. Through their hormones, they charge the body with a tension that is first and foremost of a physiological nature. The psychic representative of this tension is called "libido."

Translated, the word means: hunger, desire, particularly sexual desire. The assumption is that libido provides life with the actual tension, and all forces, strivings and desires originate in this tension. The origin of every pursuit and desire, therefore, resides within the individual, within his body, within the cells of his body, within the cells of his sexual glands. He who strives, strives as a result of his libido, therefore from an inner necessity and not because something seems worth striving for. He who desires is being pushed, not pulled. That which pulls is incidental. It would not pull or excite if there had not been a surplus of libido. All this means that what is there is of no importance, for it does not belong to us. Even if the fundamental philosophical nature of the concept of libido is apparent from this reasoning, reading what happens when the owner of these cell groups fails to completely "drain off" his libido makes its nature more obvious. He becomes ill as a result of too much tension. This means: everyone who does not have his fling, is ill. He who lives in celibacy is ill. He who becomes a widower is ill. The unmarried are ill; it is inconceivable that they will get over their physiology. It is true that he can camouflage his illness, for instance, by directing his surplus libido toward substituting objects. He can take care of a dog, look after a garden, build a house. He can write poetry, devote himself to science. All this for as long as his surplus libido lasts; spending it all means the end of poetry, science, house, garden and dog. This entire theory has been seriously defended in numerous publications. A psychiatry was even constructed upon the assumption that he who does not have his fling is ill.

Is there any reality to support this theory? Even outward

appearances are not in favor of it. Countless unmarried people are in good health. Science, art and hobbies are not examples of acts of violence upon another desire, which is supposed to be real because it originates from cells. Physiology is certainly not a factor that may be ignored, yet it is a factor determined by life itself. How much passion is within us is not dictated by a gland but by the context of life.[3] Those who were confined in concentration camps lost all sexual urge suddenly, and certainly not because groups of cells were immediately undernourished. Sexual urges became meaningless, even dangerous. All this means is that the libido-theory is a philosophy that alienates man from his environment. Only another philosophy can do away with the strange theory and provide us with a new insight into the meaning of our patients' complaints. Let us give an illustration of this.

In the limited but meaningful medical publication by Weiszäcker,[4] *Studien zur Pathogenese*, is a record of a patient suffering from *diabetes insipidus*. Her complaint is thirst, an elementary and strong desire for water, more or less comparable to that other elementary compelling desire called libido. The patient relates her complaints as follows: "I feel related to water. I go swimming whenever and wherever it is possible. I often think how delicious it must be to feel a strong squirt of water on my neck. I like streams, that is why I love going to the *Schwarzwald*. Whenever I am there, I look for a track along a stream. The water is so clear there." That she is ill,

3. As far as I know, Alfred Adler was the first to make such a statement (*Zur Kritik der Freudschen Sexual theorie des Seelenlebens*, 1911). On other aspects, too, Adler developed original reasonings that are only now fully appreciated.
4. V. von Weizsäcker, *Studien zur Pathogenese*. Wiesbaden, 1946.

different, suffering from thirst, is manifest to her, above all, in her deviating perceptions. Water plays a predominant part in her observations. She sees water more often, hears streams more often and enjoys a bath more intensively than a healthy person. She feels herself (so she says) related to water and insofar as she does she expresses a subjective condition. Yet this subjective condition remains empty if it is not exemplified objectively. She goes swimming wherever it is possible. She loves streams along the track. She would have given a poor report of her complaints if she had only related her subjective complaints. She affords insight into her condition by stating how objects look to her.

In this way, a new "pathography" is coming into existence which does not confine itself to a summary of what the patient observes "in himself," introspectively, but which consists of a description of the pathological physiognomy of objects.[5] This means describing qualities of objects that are, to the patient himself, the most real and convincing.

A person who, in the morning after a restless night, finds himself ill and decides to stay in bed for the day can, if invited to do so, report on his condition by stating how he feels subjectively: tired, nauseated, without appetite and with a head-ache—data which seem subjective but which, in reality, can hardly be called that. For one feels tiredness in legs and head, nausea in the throat, no appetite in relation to a cracker, etc. To express a strictly subjective complaint, a complaint pertaining to the subject and not to the body or its environment, is beyond our powers. He who complains, complains about things there, in the body or in the objects there. Even when

5. The word is derived from Erwin Straus.

thinking itself fails, what fails is the thinking about matters present somewhere else. Thus the patient only arrives at a real description of his condition when he relates what the wallpaper looks like, what the sound of the telephone is like and how the noise of cars outside penetrate his bedroom. To be ill, according to Madame Pastorelli,[6] who, because of a heart condition, is confined to her bed where she is to die, means first and foremost that the surroundings have changed. It means that even one's closest friends have become distant. It means that things have changed—the same things that are evidence of his health to the healthy person. "Ever since I knew," writes Jacqueline van der Waals,[7] who knows she is going to die, "the abundance, the beauty and the sweetness of the things around me are twice as sweet and lovely." To be ill, even with just a trivial illness, as much as with a mortal illness, means, above all, to experience things in a different way, to be different yonder, to live in another, maybe hardly different, maybe completely different, world.

The psychiatric patient, more often than any other, states this spontaneously. The depressed patient speaks of a world gone gloomy and dark. The flowers have lost their color, the sun has lost its brightness, everything looks dull and dead. One of my patients even went so far as to buy stronger light bulbs because the light in his room had become less bright. The patient suffering from mania, on the other hand, finds things full of color and beauty, more beautiful than he ever saw before. The schizophrenic patient sees, hears and smells indications of a world disaster. In objects, he observes the

6. F. Pastorelli, *Servitude et grandeur de la maladie*. Paris, 1933.
7. Jacqueline E. van der Waals, *Laatste verzen*. Rotterdam, 1950.

downfall of his existence. In the voices of people, in the blow-
ing of the wind, he hears that a revolution is about to come.
In the taste of his bread, he discerns evil penetrating the things
of the world. Would the psychiatrist do justice to these observations and to his patient if he should declare that the subject
is ill and that the observations of his patient are suffering from
an exaggerated use of metaphors, *from projection*? The patient
is ill; this means that *his world* is ill, literally that *his objects
are ill*, however unusual this may sound. When the psychiatric
patient tells what his world looks like, he states, without de-
tours and without mistakes, what he is like.

Let us go back to our patient of this book. He says that the
houses look old and dilapidated. He observes that they are
about to collapse; they lean over and threaten to crush him.
His complaint should be taken seriously. That is what the
street in which the patient walks is like. It is nothing like the
street as we know it, but this only means that the patient is ill
and we are not. Nothing gives us a right to hold our own observation to be truer than the patient's. Our own observation,
too, just proves what we are like and what we are. If we find
unanimity among our opinion and the opinions of countless
others, it only means that the people around us are mentally
sound and that they have grown up in the same culture. For
if a Tibetan or a pygmy should walk the same street, he, too,
in spite of his sound condition, would see another street. We
need not go that far from home. The farmer, the fisherman
and the factory workers of our own country see different
streets when they walk this one. The woman, the man, the
child, the adolescent and the aged person also observe different
streets. They see their age, their background, their upbringing,
their sex, their occupation and their intelligence; they see all

their own qualities and characteristics in the street around them. The subject's qualities are the aspects of a world, physiognomies of the objects of everyday existence. I shall go into the onesidedness of this never sufficiently emphasized conclusion later. Our patient relates how things appear to him. His existence is about to disintegrate; everything around him is old and dilapidated. He is living with the relics of a past time, and he is a living anachronism. That the streets and squares seem fearfully wide and empty is the literal expression of his "subjective," i.e., personal, condition. He is a lonely individual; the objects are far away and hostile. There is no better way for him to describe his condition: he tells the truth of his mental illness. *He is right.*

Thus, it is neither necessary nor indicated for the psychiatrist to take the side of the patient's relatives and acquaintances. He takes the side of the patient. He puts himself in the patient's existence, *in his world.* The judgment of relatives and acquaintances is generally a condemnation. But the psychiatrist's judgment also suffers from this ailment, as appears from the words denoting the symptoms: a dictionary full of rejections, however kindly they are intended. The patient is called *black-biled* (melancholic); his state of mind is a deficient variety of the sound state of mind. Or *unrestrained*: his behavior lacks the adequate restraining influences of the sound, perfect existence. One speaks of *hyperaesthesia,* of *hyperkinesia,* of *hyperthymia* and of *hypobulia, hypomnesia* and *hyprosexia.* The patient suffers from either too much or too little, he sins in proportions, he is the offense in person. The condemnation is still more obvious with words like *dementia, amorality,* perversity, *paralogia* and hallucination.

The patient consisted of mistakes. He *projected,* which

sound people only do as an exception and would rather not do at all. Is all this not related to the times in which the psychiatric patient was condemned and confined? No doubt, the institutions, hospitals and clinics in which the patient resided, have changed and improved. Does it not seem fair, then, as a result of a more righteous train of thought, also to make some improvements where the terminology is concerned? The word "projection," for instance. That the patient differs from the sound person is not important; that is obvious, even to the layman. Neither is it very important to know in what respect he differs from the sound person, assuming that this "in what respect" can be explained (the concept "projection" doesn't help much). It is important to know what his existence is like. Instead of negative, *pathography* should be positive, for in the sense meant here, the patient lives just as positively as we do.

2. MAN AND BODY

When the French physician La Mettrie[8] fell at the siege of Freiburg in the 1840's, he noticed that the fever not only changed the condition of his body but that which he had learned to call his soul as well. After that moment, his trust in the strict separation of body and soul diminished. On this subject, he wrote a book which was burnt in Paris and which made him lose his job as an army physician. Everyone thought it a disgraceful book, not only because of its deriding tone, but, above all, because they felt that the author had been denying a sacred principle—the principle that man has a material and mortal body, and a soul that is neither material nor mortal.

8. J. O. De La Mettrie, *Histoire maturelle de l'ame* (later called *Traite de l'ame*). The Hague, 1745.

This supposition, which was difficult to question on philosophical ground to start with, seemed a law from a theological point of view. People were wrong, though. In any case, the separation is not a biblical one; the word "immortal" appears only twice in the Bible, and on both occasions it applies to God. According to the Bible, we are mortal, totally; we might say "body and soul," but this distinction is not made in the Bible. Through Christ's death, eternity was granted to us, mortals, but that is not the same thing. We are not concerned here with these distinctions, however important they may be.

What is under discussion now is the psychological significance of La Mettrie's experience, which experience can be repeated by anyone inclined to do so. A person whose brain suffers is different *himself*. He hears differently, thinks differently, feels differently, believes differently; there is nothing, really, that is not changed by the fever. Can such a strict distinction—body and soul—be correct, then? We should realize that, in this distinction, the soul is the essential part of us; the body, the cover of this essential part, is an extraneous matter. The body does not belong to oneself. Is this real? To begin with a crude example: does a person who is known to be suffering from cancer say that the disease is just striking his cover and thus leaves himself unaffected? Does the mother who, in dismay, strokes the arm of her sick child, believe that she is touching a jail which contains her child? Or does her hand touch her child? What does the young woman who is attending to her body think? Does she think she is attending to an object (called body), an obstacle between her and the world, between her and other people, or does she think she is attending to *herself*? A person needs only to look at his hand to know that he is there himself, in this hand. Legion are the instances that make it clear that we *are* our bodies.

We are not inclined to deny it, even if we say that we also *have* bodies. There is no doubt about this, either. A simple example: A person looking in the mirror notes that he *has* such a face with such ears and such a nose. He can, if he should conceive it, cut off his ear and throw it from him with the words: I used to have it and now I *have* it no longer. It must be admitted that this example is not common, far less common than those of *being* our body. The statement of having such a face, this nose and this chin is not common, either. Even by saying that he has a body, a person withdraws himself to a certain extent from everyday existence. By saying this, he also changes his body a little. For the body one has is unlike the body one is. The body one has, has been left, more or less, by its owner. A distance must be effected, however small, between oneself and one's body before one is able to state "I have a body."

Talking about one's body means talking about oneself. A person washes *himself*, not his body. He shaves *himself*, not his face. And if he is shaving his *chin*, he is not shaving the chin of the face he has, but of the face he is. He who is cutting his nails is cutting *his* nails; not for a moment does he estrange himself from his hand, unless there is something wrong with it. A disturbance, a disease, has to enter the body one *is* to make the body one *has* come into existence. Or one has to reflect upon the body one *is* for the body one *has* to come into existence.

With these words appears a peculiarity which was observed in a similar form in the discussion of the relationship of man and world. It became clear there that *reflection* creates a distance between man and world, a distance *prereflectively* unknown in everyday life. Prereflectively, man and body are very closely related, if not identical, while simple reflection originates the conviction that the body belongs to the world of material objects. And this conviction, that the body is an object, appeared to be extraordinarily fertile to medical science. For an object one *has* can be dissected, *and in this way* one can try to understand it, whereas that which *is* cannot be dissected.

The medical student who is caressing his girlfriend's hand makes a mistake if, in his mind, he simultaneously goes over his anatomy. His girlfriend's hand has no blood vessels, muscles, nerves or bones. He is caressing another hand—which is indeed soft and hard here and there and has a number of features (even throbbing vessels) that cannot be found in his anatomy book. Even the physiologist knows that it is not correct, that it is not fitting at a festive dinner table to speculate on the fate of the food he is eating with other people. No chemical processes are taking place in his stomach: he notices that he becomes satisfied. Prereflective life, that is, life as it is lived in our day-to-day existence, has no knowledge of physiology. Eating, one becomes stomach, just as one *becomes* head, studying—head to such an extent that the hungry stomach does not exist, nor do the tired, crossed legs under the table. In the sexual act, it is not the sexual organs, objects, that are made available to one another, two subjects jailed in their bodies; the mere thought makes the sexual act impossible. In the sexual act, man and woman become creatures of sex, even sexual organs—a change about which the anatomist and the physiologist can establish nothing at all. The matters with which they deal belong to another order, to the order of reflective, therefore, gnostic knowledge, whereas the transformation of the man's and the woman's bodies belongs to the order of prereflective, therefore, pathic experience.

So the prereflective body (which we are) certainly has organs —stomach, head, sexual organs, hand, eyes, ear, etc., even blood vessels—but these organs are not identical with those of the books on anatomy and physiology.

In medical psychology and psychosomatic medicine, it is known that the psychological complaints of psychiatric patients cannot be examined by means of a normal medical examination, because a normal examination is directed toward organs that are not meant by the patient. When the gastric-ulcer patient complains about his stomach, he does not mean the organ anatomically described there just under his diaphragm called stomach, *ventriculus*, or better still, *saccus digestivus*, which means digestive pouch. He means the other organ which, when he eats, receives and digests. *His* stomach. "To eat," from a prereflective point of view, is to receive, to savor or to devour. Even "to digest" has a prereflective meaning: of assimilating in general, of making merge with what one is, even of declaring oneself in agreement with the events and incidents of life as such a person who eats accepts his life, even if he does so aggressively. The gastric-ulcer patient cannot accept his life. He feels inadequate, and he finds no opportunity enabling him to feel adequate. So he digests himself and eats a hole in his stomach, a hole that also becomes visible in that other organ meant by the anatomist. This example does not pretend to be generally valid. Some gastric patients get their ulcers in other ways. The point here is to make clear that the psychopathologists and the anatomist are not speaking of the same organ, stomach, and that it would be good if one could give a description of what is meant by the word "prereflective" stomach. This is not entirely impossible. There is even a school of thought in psychosomatic medicine that has made the prereflective its emphasis.[9]

A second example, also from the field of psychosomatics. The patient suffering from high blood pressure without diseased organs or organ systems complains about a tenseness of his whole body. He *is bursting out of his vessels,* but the vessels of the anatomy book are not the ones that are about to burst. His "prereflective" vessels are under pressure: the vessels anyone knows when the blood rises to his head, or when one becomes pale with fright or red with hatred or annoyance. These vessels' walls have something to do with the limits of shame and impulsiveness, walls against which aggression collides. Aggression is a matter of the body. The person who relaxes every muscle, who removes every tension from his body, cannot be aggressive. Shame does not exist as a purely psychic quality. Shame is, as Madame Guyon expressed it, that which envelops the body like clothes. Shame resides in the walls of the body. All so-called purely psychic qualities are qualities or conditions of the body. The gentle person moves unlike an audacious person. An aggressive person's voice is loud, his muscles are tense, his blood flows faster through his vessels. Thus the restrained aggression, the ag-

9. The best, even (to my taste) unsurpassed example, of this remains: V. von Weizsäcker, *Fälle und Probleme, Anthropologische Vorlesungen in der medizinischen Klinik.* Stuttgart, 1947.

gression which is to be kept within limits, is also a quality of the body, which can be named *hypertension*. The essential, or rather, *prereflective*, *hypertension* can then perhaps also be established with a sphygmomanometer and may result in a bursting of an anatomical vessel. Also, in this example, I do not intend to find a general rule applicable to all cases of hypertension; I am only trying to find illustrations of the distinction between the body of the anatomy books (which we have) and the body of nongnostic, pathic, prereflective life (which we are).

The patient in this book is not suffering from a psychosomatic disturbance in the strictest sense of the word. At a thorough medical examination, no defects were found. This means that his illness is not organically physical to such an extent that it has resulted in organic defects. But let us not consider the distinction between organic and nonorganic neurotic disturbances. What is more important is what both categories have in common—that the patient's physical complaint concerns his prereflective body. The patient of this book is convinced that his heart is diseased. The cardiologist states that there are no defects. His statement makes little impression upon the patient. The reason is obvious, now: physician and patient speak of different organs. The physician is thinking of a hollow muscle, furnished with valves and a septum. The patient speaks of the heart, which can be in the right place; for him, his heart had left the right place. He speaks of the heart that can be broken by a gesture or a glance, whereas the pathologist does not find a trace of a defect. The patient means the heart that can be quite all right even when the cardiologist finds it defective. And which can be diseased even when all physicians declare that it functions splendidly. To say, then, that the patient "is physically expressing an emotional conflict" is to confuse two realities. He who says that the patient is converting, meaning conveying from one order to another, forgets that the patient is not speaking of the organs meant by the physician, and that he is not converting, not conveying anything from one sphere into another as he keeps speaking within the order of one reality, which he characterized by the fact that the distinction between body and soul has not been made. The patient does have a diseased heart, he is not mistaken. Neither is he deluding himself; he is suffering from a serious heart condition; for the heart he means is the center of his world. That this center is disturbed, as the patient says, no one can doubt. His heart became cold. Yet not entirely cold. It is rebelling. It is beating restlessly against his chest. The patient also complains about a weakness of his legs and about a defective equilibrium. That the neurologist finds no defects will no longer surprise anyone. His reflex hammer does not reach the legs meant by the patient. His legs fail him in another, more general, context. He has lost the ability to stand, literally; in the same sense, his equilibrium is disturbed. He is about to fall; the fall also occurs when the legs of the anatomy books fail him. But this is not necessary. His existence itself is *to fall*. Even when he is lying down, he is falling.

The analysis of his physical complaints is not concluded with this. The reader can guess what the patient's tiredness means. His headache. What matters here is only the form of explanation. What should not be forgotten, though, is the following.

Comparing the results of the investigation into the nature

of the patient's world with that which has just been observed about his body, one establishes a relationship, if not a similarity. The patient says that the houses are old and dilapidated and are about to collapse upon him. His world is collapsing. Is he not saying the same thing when he states that his legs are failing him and he feels as if he is losing his sense of equilibrium! *World* and *body* are interrelated. Then the customary distinction of *world* and *body* is probably much too definite.

Even in 1935, Buytendijk and Plessner[10] propounded that the physical behavior of man and animal could not be understood unless the question, in what sort of world do man and animal exist, has been answered. The authors then describe the physical behavior of a response; they compare the relation of body and world to a dialogue. I shall try to clarify this concept with a few examples.

A young girl has an evening off. She decides to go into the city and hopes to attract the attention of the boys she will see. She puts on her best dress and applies some makeup. When she is ready, she examines the result in the mirror, or, rather she has other people, seeing through her eyes, look at the girl in the mirror. If these other people say, "Does she not look pretty," she gets up, and for a moment or two, trips about in her room. *She is in the city already, then*; otherwise, she could not walk like that, nor could she look so sexy. Then she leaves her room and says goodbye to her parents. She behaves differently, saying goodbye. She walks in another way, and she does not even think of a daring look. Her parents are not necessarily critical where her behavior is concerned. She is not restraining or correcting herself, she is just behaving naturally; the change

10. F. J. J. Buytendijk and H. Plessner, *Acta Biotheoretica*, A, I, 1935.

in her behavior is effected without effort. This means that, during the moments of saying goodbye, she is still situated in her childhood surroundings to such an extent that her behavior is adjusted to them. Her body gives a corresponding response to what her parental home is shouting at her: "You are a child!" Then she leaves. As soon as she is in the city, other words are reaching her: the streets are glittering with a light she never saw when she was a child. This is evidence of her maturity to her. The way people look at her tells that she is dressed like a young woman and that she has a mature body. Again her body responds: it trips about and looks sexy.

Why is a soldier supposed to stand in a symmetrical position[11] when he presents himself for duty? Because the order he receives has only one meaning and not two or three meanings or a number of half-meanings. If the soldier were slouching on one leg, he could be given half an order. But his world is not like that. As a soldier, he does not live an existence of maybe yesses or maybe nos but in the world of this way and no other way. Why, within the memory of man, is the attitude of prayer a symmetrical one? Because the world of the praying person, too, though differing from that of the soldier, has a direction, a direction without conditions, without roundabout ways. He who prays, is praying, expelling all maybes of the things around him for a moment; or rather, that is what he is trying to do. Why is the attitude of an adolescent asymmetrical? Because in his world there is nothing permanent; everything is dubious and there is no direction.

The body adjusts itself, is what I wrote. The words are not

11. F. J. J. Buytendijk, *Algemene theorie der menselijke houding en beweging.* Utrecht, 1948.

correct yet, for that which is adjusting is second, it reacts. In the relation of body and world, neither of the two is second. The body forms itself[12] in accordance with the world in which its task lies. It takes on a form, a figure: a working figure, a fighting figure, a loving figure. But one is equally justified in saying that the world is changed by the body moving about in it. Objects take on different shapes, working shapes, fighting shapes, loving shapes. Do objects not look different to the fighter and to the peaceful person? Objects *are different* to them. Thus, prereflective body and prereflective world are united as in a dialogue. Both should be understood within their context.

Of this context, a few psychiatric examples. First, the almost motionless catatonic patient. When the symptoms of the disease are completely developed, the patient does not speak a word and he keeps standing, entirely without movement, in the same spot. He does not reply to questions. His expression is fixed and gloomy. He seems to be full of thoughts, while, at the same time, one wonders if he is thinking at all. He is an enigma. Only after a long period does one become aware, through meaningful trivialities, that much is penetrating his mind and that he appreciates a hello even if he never responds. His immovability results in swollen legs. Then he is led to bed to prevent circulation troubles, but imperturbably, he returns to the spot of his preference. Thus he stands for weeks, years, sometimes many years, in complete rest. From where comes his motionlessness? There are no physical defects. *The patient lives in another world.* The sound person's world is

12. V. E. von Gebsattel," "Süchtiges Verhalten im Gebiet sexueller Verirrungen," *Monatschrift für Psychiatrie und Neurologie*, 1932.

characterized by direction, utility and purpose. For everyone, the streetcar, standing at a stop, has the meaning of a *means of conveyance, going from-to*, even if starting point and finish are unknown. The streetcar has purpose, direction and utility. That is how we see it. The flowers in the living room are adornment of the room. They are just beginning to bloom, or they are about to wither; our seeing measures the length of time they will remain fresh. Everything has time, future and past. Even the block of rock, seemingly eternal, is tertiary, or diluvial, or it originates from creation. Really, there is nothing not provided with time. Everything lasts. If we should take duration away from objects, they would look different. In this sense, things are different for the catatonic patient. His time is different. He lives in another time. If he is asked what year it is, he might mention the year in which his psychoses began. He has not grown older since then; time stopped flowing. To him, no buds grow into flowers, nor is there a streetcar going from-to. Just so little is he aware of utility and purpose. It is useless to ask him the purpose of the flowers in the living room. Every change or shifting of objects is meaningless, obscure, unnecessary, not really possible. Nothing really changes, no one really moves. All things are frozen in a sort of timeless space. That is what his world is like. The body responds to this world by not moving. The catatonic patient stands like a statue in a museum of oddities.

For the sound person, the world is so much time from-to and consequently movement that his body moves as well. Is the world fast, that is, do objects vibrate, does everything indicate restlessness and progress? Then the body also races. Does everything have time, do objects suggest restfulness, do they,

59

A DIFFERENT EXISTENCE

perhaps, show their mark of eternity? Then the movement also becomes slow. The city dweller rushes, the farmer moves steadily, the monk is solemn in the way he moves. Their objects are different.

For the patient suffering from morbid melancholy, particularly for the endogenous depressive patient, life moves very slowly. He sees everything jogging along laboriously; therefore, his body, too, moves slowly and laboriously. The world looks lifeless and withering; therefore, he feels tired, dull and inactive.

For the patient suffering from the morbid liveliness of a mania, however, life proceeds easily, there are no obstacles, everything gives to his movements; consequently, he moves freely and fast. His world is very much alive, colorful and fresh. That is why he also feels fresh and alive; he feels so light that he almost gets the idea that he can fly.[13]

The schizophrenic, finally, sees hardly doubtful indications of the world's destruction. He smells damnation and observes the work of satanic powers. Is it surprising that he complains about an abnormal body? His thoughts are cut off, and he is manipulated by machinery. He feels it. He moves like it. His body moves in a mannered way in a strange, insecure world.

Thus the separation of *body* and *world* is less strict than the Cartesian train of thought suggests. The following paragraph intends to show that even more distinctions have been made too rigorously in this train of thought.

3. MAN AND FELLOWMAN, COMMUNICATION

When the mother of the Jewish girl, the central character of "Het huisje aan de sloot" (the Cabin at the Ditch), by Carry

13. L. Binswanger, *Ueber Ideenflucht*. Zürich, 1933.

van Bruggen, on the morning of the sabbath, takes from the
table the daily red and black cloth and puts the gleaming white
one in its place, then, writes Carry van Bruggen (no doubt
from her own experience), there is always one undetermined
moment in which "it" happens, a moment one always missed.
As long as the black and red cloth remains on the table, there
is nothing; mother comes, and there is nothing extraordinary
about her, either. She takes away the black and red cloth;
the bare table is old, full of stains and scratches. Now the
white cloth flutters in mother's hand, by the lamp, almost
touching it; now it is lowered, it is on the table and—another
miss. "It" has come and no one has seen "it" arrive. Mother
suddenly has another face; and every chair and the cabinet
and the stove—they all look different. No one has been able to
see the actual change, no one has been able to catch that
moment. But next time, the little girl decides again and again,
she won't be looking at the cloth; but she'll watch her mother
and the cabinet, the chairs and the stove, for one day she
wants to catch this wonderful moment in which all things
change their appearance.

In which all things change their appearance? What does
the author mean to say? That the objects change their appearance? Their shape? She speaks of the *change in themselves* of the objects. Yet this kind of change has never been
observed. The observation of the change itself is a difficult-to-
establish fact. The change in itself is a fact. Are objects capable
of change, then? Of this, the author is entirely convinced, as
we are when the same sort of incident happens to us. Each one
of us has a memory similar to the one of the girl of the story.
An experience. Or is it more correct to say that every day each
one of us lives in the reality of this kind of experience? Ob-

jects are changing their appearance daily, continuously and never without reason. Of this, another example, also derived from Carry van Bruggen's book.

The mother is sitting behind the house. As she is scraping carrots, she is singing a song of which she only knows the first lines. "My beloved Spain, land of my ancestors, my beloved Spain, land where I live." Again and again, the same lines. The reader is invited to imagine the scene. When the mother fetches another bunch of carrots, she is gone for a moment. Just now, when mother stopped singing to get another bunch, all the things—the house, the sky, the tree— were different, almost as if they were not there at all. If one wanted to know whether all these things were still there, one had to take a good look; but when mother returned and resumed her singing, "My beloved Spain," everything was there quite naturally.

Things change to such an extent that they disappear and return. The house, the sky, the tree, the chair, the cabinet and the stove, everything changes. But nothing ever changes without sense or reason. Objects change on special occasions. When someone arrives or leaves. When the day begins, or when the evening falls. On Sunday, things look different from their appearance on workdays. When I know that my friend will not come, the bottle of Médoc changes. This is not the difficulty; the difficulty lies in the *seeing* of the change. A closer inspection does not show anything.

Two ways of reasoning are open to the psychologist, and the psychiatrist with him, depending on how he interprets the fact that objects change. One, the psychologist believes in the observations of the closer inspection. Then he will observe nothing. He denies the change and interprets what is happening as a projection—after which he shall have to explain what projection means. He is unable to give such an explanation. In the other way, the psychologist does not believe in the observation of the closer inspection. He will say, then, that how we see at a closer inspection is not how the person who saw the change was seeing, and consequently, it is not how the psychologist should look if he wants to understand this seeing

The psychologist, the psychiatrist, of the latter way of thinking desire to restrict themselves definitely to what is really happening. The psychologist makes every effort to prevent his science from being disturbed. He tries to describe phenomena *as they are.* He is a *phenomenologist;* that is, he respects what is put on record, the incidents just as they are occurring. So he has to respect the observation of the incidents, the seeing of the incident's objects. He disturbs the objects by closer inspections, so he refrains from inspecting them. Which does not mean that, in the future, he will see superficially. On the contrary, he is of the opinion that by not submitting things to a closer inspection he will be able to see them more clearly and more accurately.

A closer inspection (in the sense meant here) reduces things to those that can be observed without emotion. Daily observances do not occur, or occur only seldom, without emotion. Therefore, those who look closely see other matters. He who desires to know what, in a given situation, is happening psychologically, does well *to put himself in that situation.* He should refrain from quickly pronouncing judgment on the situation, for a quick judgment is usually premature. First to describe, then to judge. To describe is the most important. An accurate description of an incident necessarily involves a judgment concerning the incident, *according to a theory of the incident. Only then, if needed, is a theory on the incident permitted.* The first theory is the one of the incident and of the actor in it. The first psychopathology: the patient's. Well, then, he who puts himself in the place of the patient, in his situation, in his observation (that is, in his objects), sees the objects differently, the streets, the houses, the stones. He who puts himself in the place of Carry van Bruggen's girl sees objects disappearing and returning. For this is what the girl sees. The investigator adheres to the given facts. This is the basic principle of all phenomenology: *the investigator remains true to the facts as they are happening.*

On this principle, no theory can be built that justifies the concept of projection. *No one experiences projection.* No one experiences the parting of something subjective from oneself, which then adheres to amorphous matter, which in turn consequently becomes an object. The objects are objects, immediately. He who sees does not see nothing at first and only then, after his projection, an object. There is no free interval between the seeing before and the seeing after the projection, which free interval could, according to the theory, be expected certainly when a projection changes nameless objects into things that can be used and savored. That projection, which would take place too quickly and not consciously enough to be noticed and put on record, remains an hypothesis. If there is a free interval, then it can only be expected after and not before the seeing of the objects. One sees the objects and establishes loneliness, not the other way around, as the doctrine of projection presupposes.

Another example to illustrate the significance of the objects in the person-to-person relation. In "De verborgen bron" (The Hidden Well), by Hella Haasse, a man writes to his wife about his experiences during a visit to the house they have just inherited. He is enthusiastic about what he has seen, and in his delight, he writes, "I wish you were here!" Then he remembers the gulf separating them and continues, "But no, I don't wish that, probably because I would be afraid of seeing things with your eyes." Let us suppose that the man had not corrected himself and that his wife, at his request, had accompanied him on a visit to this house, so much liked by him. If we are to believe the author, he would have seen the house *with other eyes*. The house would, because she was looking with him, have changed. It would have become less attractive, less inviting, less habitable. We have reason to believe the author. We all know people in whose company we would prefer not to go shopping, not to visit a museum, not to look at a landscape, because we would like to keep these things undamaged. Just as we all know people in whose company it is pleasant to take a walk because the objects encountered come to no harm. These people we call friends, good companions, loved ones.

Summarizing: A word, a look or a gesture can brighten things or make them gloomy. The person with us is not another isolated individual, next to us, who throws words in our ear and who remains foreign to the objects around us. He is the person who is either with us or not with us and who makes the degree of togetherness or distance visible in objects, concretely and in reality. Togetherness is no mere idea. Togetherness or distance appears within the physiognomy of the world. This physionomy can be trusted or disturbed, can be near or far. When the mother of Carry van Bruggen's girl went away, the objects disappeared; when she returned, they were back where they had been. More reality is impossible. Togetherness is no illusion, no psychism.

That the other person frequently *enlarges* the distance to objects (to the object or to the *task*—the *task* is always a more or less inviting or compelling aspect of the object) has been convincingly illustrated by the French phenomenologist Jean-Paul Sartre. Here is one of his illustrations.

A man is looking through a keyhole at scenes not meant for his eye. He is absorbed by what he sees. He has, as it were, entered the room through the keyhole (the phenomenologist is prepared to take this almost literally). He has left his body outside the door; that is why he hardly notices how tired it is getting. Then he hears footsteps approaching. Suddenly several things happen. Before he has even started to straighten himself, the room on the other side of the door, the room he was in, disappears. He is back at the outside of the keyhole. That which had been near, so near that he became absorbed in it, to the extent that he was unaware of his body, becomes —as a result of the presence of another person—far, very far indeed. The distance remains if he finds that the other person disapproves of his conduct. But possibly the footsteps are those of a person who has often looked through this keyhole with him. Immediately, the nearness of the scene returns; the scene may come even nearer as a result of the joint experience.

These examples are attempts to clarify the nature of the contact between man and the fellowman. Although they are common enough, in this context they have a peculiar aspect.

Instead of illustrating a connection *between people*, these examples illustrate changes in nearness or distance to *objects*. But this is connected with the other phenomenological interpretation of human contact. As long as psychology is based on a philosophical interpretation considering the existence of the soul to be locked within the body, psychology could not be expected to be concerned with objects. For objects are foreign to us; they are outside our body and can only, to a certain extent, be incorporated when our desire, our lust or *libido* is discharged into them. In other words: the objects never really belong to us, for that which we consider the objects' intimate or trusted aspects always finally belong to the subject. Until recently, this has been the explanation given by psychology. The world was of no significance. In accordance with this view, the contact between people had to be found in a connection between them. But this "between" remained empty. A statement about what exists between people necessarily contains observations on objects, duties, interests, plans, to put it briefly, on what is *there, yonder. Between*, there is nothing. Even an exchange of looks is aimed at *yonder*. Phenomenological psychology originates from this observation. There is an original contact with objects. We often even *are* the objects. The shoemaker loses awareness of himself; he is absorbed in his work, he becomes the shoe he is repairing—if not, he might just as well stop working. The writer becomes his problem; he gets into his problem, and he liberates himself when he solves it. When we realize this, we avoid trying to find the contact between man and fellow man in a connection between "souls." The poverty of the last word implies the impossibility of the preceding one. There is no "between." Interhuman relations manifest themselves as physionomies of a world, as nearness or distance of duties or plans, *of objects.*

Yet this answer cannot be complete. There is yet another contact between man and fellow man. We shake hands; we put a hand on a person's shoulder or touch his arm when we want his attention. We look at one another, and we understand one another with a wink. People in love hold hands. There is an embrace, a kiss, a caress. The essence of all these phenomena is not the contact of anonymous bodies. The contact is a contact between man and fellow man, direct, indivisible, a taking part in one another. A handshake can elucidate the nature of a contact as such. Everyone knows the handshake that depreciates, abuses and insults; then there is the large category of handshakes signifying friendship or love. Whatever all this means and whatever marginal notes could be made about it, there is a directly physical, directly interhuman contact that *does not refer to objects.* What does this signify to the phenomenologist? As always, the answer can only be found by means of a concrete example.

When I observe the back of my hand,[14] I see veins that show a certain configuration. The configurations on left and right hands differ. When I look at other persons' hands, I see configurations again. No two persons have hands with the same configuration. These patterns are like fingerprints; no two persons have the same print of the skin furrows of their fingertips. Everything about us is personal. Every part differs from the same part of any other person. Why this individual element? Of course, the veins on the back of the hand have to follow some course or another; they are there, they are necessary and

14. An example derived from J.-P. Sartre, L'être et le néant. Paris, 1943.

they have to be somewhere. But why are they lying just there and nowhere else? Why, moreover, do their configurations differ on one's left and right hands? Why, finally, does the configuration differ with every person? The veins would function just as well if they had another configuration. Then why are they located as they are? No one knows a satisfactory answer. Yet everyone knows the answer. As soon as one caresses this "incidental" hand, the conviction is born that the veins are lying just as they should. The caress removes the incidental nature of the configuration. The caress turns the hand into the hand that had to be there.

A caress brings about a change in the hand. A caress transforms the body, even if the physiologist is unable to report on this transformation. As individuals, we all feel our own bodies as more or less foreign to us. A body has a certain shape, which was neither requested nor desired; and it has certain peculiarities. Even if we have to accept its shape and peculiarities as we accept the weather, we still distrust it. Why this particular body? This nose? This forehead? But then, another person teaches us that this body is exactly right. In friendship and in love, the incidental nature of the body is eliminated; a justification of the body takes place. Love removes the distance between bodies, something like adhesion occurs, one begins to occupy one's body and is invited to *be* that body.

The other person plays a part in one's relationship to one's body. He can make the relationship closer. He can enlarge the distance. Of the one as well as of the other, there are numerous instances. The girl with freckles lives on strained terms with her face, until a man lets her know that he loves her as she is, with her freckles. Perhaps he tells her that he loves her because of her freckles, whereas so many girls have to do without them. That is what love is like. Love springs from peculiarities that can be found only in the loved person. The exceptional peculiarity, even if, as a result of the opinion of others, it had become an obstacle, can be the basis on which one is accepted.

In a preceding paragraph, we discussed the man who looks through the keyhole. At the moment he hears footsteps, the room is taken from him. But there is more. At the same moment, a distance is created between him and his body. He takes over the condemning look from the other person, and through the latter's eye (the phenomenologist takes it literally) he sees and condemns that body.

Words, gestures and looks of others can enlarge or minimize the distance between man and body. Frequently, there is a mixture of both. Of this, an example.

A girl of about sixteen enters the room in which her elder brother is talking to a few friends. When his friends see who is coming in, they stop talking and look at her. For the first time in her life, the girl notices that she is being seen through male eyes. She blushes. What does her blushing mean? Generally speaking, there is a difference between the way in which a man and a woman look at another person. Whereas female eyes can rest on the surface of objects and people, a masculine glance is inclined to go through the objects; it penetrates, unmasks, changes, more than does the feminine glance.[15] The girl notices that she is being looked at with this kind of glance. Her brother's friends are looking at her in an unmasking way; they are looking through her clothes. Their eyes are trying to

15. F. J. J. Buytendijk, *De vrow*. Utrecht, 1951.

undress. As a result, the girl is robbed of her body; to a modest degree, her body turns into a body of her brother's friends. But this estrangement of her own body is not all. Also, for the first time in her life, she finds that she desires to possess this different, newly shaped, body. She becomes a woman entirely. Later, in a less surprising moment of her own choice, she wants to *be* this body, and to prove it, her body—those parts that are seen—is filled with blood. She blushes, becomes visible, more visible than she was before the masculine glances. Her blood goes out to meet their glances. But at the same time, her blushing is a barrier behind which she is hiding. She hides behind a layer of blood. Her blush refuses. Her blushing is the result both of estrangement from her body *and* of new intimacy with her body. The other persons' glances make her body far off and nearby.

So far, these examples, I trust, make possible the summarizing in one statement of the answer as to the nature of the relationship between man and fellow man: the relationship between man and fellow man is such that it realizes itself in the form, and in the nearness or distance, of world and body.

It seems appropriate, finally, to illustrate this definition by means of the psychology of an everyday chat. My friend and I are talking to one another. This talking involves talking about something. Just talking, without having a subject to talk about, is impossible. We are talking about Iceland, which neither of us has ever visited, but which we know from the books we read. We are not talking about the image of it created in our minds—this image is a legacy of the objectless subject—but we mean Iceland as it really is. We are talking about a real country. When my friend talks about this country, I try

71

to enter into the things he says; however inaccurate our opinions may be, I try to be in Iceland. When it is my turn to speak, he tries to be with me in Iceland. This being there, together, is our friendship. For if I had been talking to someone less sympathetic, my words, even if they were the same, would not have made us be in Iceland together. Nor would his words to me put us in Iceland. There might even have been a certain reluctance to create a common ground which, in this discussion, means real Iceland. The unreal and unshared aspect would, at that moment, have been our dislike for one another; for dislike and friendship mean *concreteness of objects*. In the talk with my friend, a real Iceland comes into existence; even if I don't know Iceland, I see it before my eyes. It is born in his words and mine. But at the same time, I see him, my friend. I see his enthusiastic expression. With my eyes, I go over his face, whose expression harmonizes with that Iceland evoked by him in my mind. In one glance, I see his body, appreciate his look, his smile, his hands. I show my appreciation to him, however vaguely expressed. My appreciation affords him the liberty of speaking as he is speaking, to look as he is looking, and to move as he is moving. My presence is no criticism of his expression but an appreciation of it. In my glance, he can be as he wishes to be. My speaking, hearing and seeing with him and my seeing of his speaking body cause an adhesion between him and his body. This adhesion between him and his body is literally the relationship between him and me: our friendship. The same applies to me. I am talking about Iceland. I am evoking it with my words, perhaps to the extent that I see it in my mind—yet I have never been there. I do not see an image; my conceptions are reaching the real country, up north. The assumption that these conceptions are aimed at an image and not at reality is, again, the product of a psychology which separates man and world. The image is a sole individual's possession, whereas this Iceland, reached and visualized through my words, is a possession of ours, my friend's and mine. That is why I am speaking so easily; that is why I am seeing so much, because my friend is hearing me. I enter this Iceland without compunction, because this friendship with my friend knows no barriers. The removal of the barriers *between me and the objects* is the friendship *between him and me.* At the same time, I know he is looking at me. He is seeing me gesticulate, talk, look. I am moving my body freely; without obstruction, I am flowing into my arms, my hands, my throat and mouth, my eyes. *I am in possession of my body;* I am this body—which implies that I am on good terms with my friend.

In the section on the relationship of man and body, it appeared that the separation of body and world should not be understood too strictly. Body and world are connected with one another. Objects invite the body to assume a form; the body forms the objects. Consequently, the changes of the world and of the body, such as are taking place in the talk, are not two occurrences independent of one another. That my friend and I are able to talk about Iceland means that he and I are able to move our bodies more freely, and the other way round. Both are one.

Now, what does all this mean for the patient of this book? He says that the objects around him have become strange. This means that he does not have right contacts with people. And he says that his body has changed; he does not trust his body and he is afraid that his heart, this center of the body, is going to fail him. With this, he states once more that he is not on good terms with people. People will be an obstacle to the ownership of his body, just as much as they are an obstacle to the ownership of a world. When he finally states that, to him, people seem like hostile wooden puppets, he expresses for the third time what the disturbance is that brings him to the therapist: he is seriously disturbed in his contacts with other people.

The patient is clear enough. What has not become clear is how the patient got into such a contact disturbance. What happened in his life to cause everyone to become his enemy? The next section is devoted to this question: we must now give attention to the relation of man and time.

What is time?

4. MAN AND TIME; LIFE HISTORY

In his *Confessiones*, Augustine puts to himself the same question, the most difficult one with which a thinker can confront himself: what is time? As soon as he tries to formulate an answer, he is in a quandary. "When someone asks me what time is," writes Augustine, "I know it, but when I try to explain I no longer know it." Time is a matter of course. Without hesitating, we see on a watch what time it is. Without fail, we localize in time an event that took place long ago. With ease, we make appointments for the days to come. Time is our possession. We live in it. We flow with it. For time flows; this we realize quite well, for even while we are asleep, it becomes later. Every day we establish that time passes quickly or slowly, without effort, without study or trouble. Time is obvious, self-evident. But if we want to know what time is, what is flowing and how it is flowing, there is no explanation.

This concerns not only time, for that matter. The same difficulty, though perhaps not to the same extent, arises with the question: what is space? Or: what is our body? Or: what is, really, the interhuman contact? None of these questions causes any difficulty in everyday life. We take possession of space: we travel, fly, enter or leave a place. We use our body as if we are this body; we move, we bathe, we lie in the sun. Without thinking, we shake hands, we talk. We have no trouble *living* the answer to these questions. As soon as we start thinking about them, however, as soon as we try to examine them, the difficulties are incalculable. Matters which, prereflectively, were clear, become obscure after reflection. Phenomenology is that extraordinary and pretentious science which tries to solve these problems prereflectively. Pretentious, for how can one think about, reflect on, that which, by definition, takes place before thinking, prereflectively? It seems an obvious impossibility.

The phenomenologist is not blind to this. He is quite aware of this difficulty—perhaps, as a result of his efforts, even more so than anyone else—but he does not want to call it an impossibility. To arrive at an explanation of prereflective matters, he will observe, one has to abandon the usual way of thinking. Instead of propounding a reflective and, as is illustrated by the history of thought, always slightly strange, artificial and therefore not quite satisfactory, theory on the stated problems, one has to make the problem speak for itself. This does not seem very clear, but in the preceding pages, a few instances have been given. When the question about the rela-

75

tionship of man and world was raised, the answer was not an argument but a description of an incident. This incident remained the dominating element. In other words, I tried to stick to the reality appearing through this incident as strictly as possible. That this is a difficult procedure is obvious. Also obvious is that one can make mistakes in this procedure. One always makes mistakes. But that is not what we are discussing. What I wish to state is that the phenomenologist is obsessed by the concrete. To observe what is happening is his first and last aim, probably more accurately defined when extended with one word: what is happening *there*. Well now, there was the bottle of wine. Let us, then, describe this bottle. This does not appear easy. It is difficult to capture a kind of "theory," which starts and ends *there*, in words. Yet if we succeed in doing this, the prereflective answer is ready.

Objects have something to say to us—this is common knowledge among poets and painters. Therefore, poets and painters are born phenomenologists. Or rather, we are all born phenomenologists; the poets and painters among us, however, are capable of conveying their views to others, a procedure also attemped laboriously, by the professional phenomenologist. We all understand the language of objects. We live in an adjusted world, in a self-evident one. The swimmer enters the water because the water is proving to him in a thousand ways that it is prepared to receive his body. The child digs into the sand because the sand cries out to it: dig! This is the way we move into a house. We see the rooms the way they will be furnished later: there the corner to sit in, there the bed for the child, there the warmth in the winter, there the coolness in the summer. There: domesticity. The house is habitable.

Phenomenology is a method; it could be called an attitude. The method is a way of observing, new in science; new, for instance, in psychology, not at all new in general life. On the contrary, the phenomenologist wants to observe in the way one usually observes. He has an unshakable faith in the everyday observation of objects, of the body, of the people around him and of time, because the answers to stated questions are based on the results of this sort of observation. On the other hand, he distrusts theoretical and objective observations, observations at a closer inspection, the kind of observations made by the physicist. He distrusts standard opinions, quickly formed opinions like projection, conversion, transference and mythicizing. He is convinced that this kind of opinion mystifies reality with an easy, but incorrect, and as a rule obscure, theory. He wishes to hold back his opinion (for he, too, has to express one) until later and listen to what the incidents, the phenomena, tell him. His science is called phenomenology. His story tries to be the interpretation of what he observes: hears, sees, smells and feels.

He wants to live and to have his psychology spring from this life. If he intends to write a discourse on swimming, he will want, first of all, to swim—and repeat his swimming until he knows and can express what swimming is. Only he who knows the sea, the river, the stream, the lake, physically can write about what it really is like. The river here, and there, the Rhine, the lake of Geneva, the Atlantic Ocean, the Mediterranean—only after having been there, can one write about it. If the phenomenologist wishes to write about driving a car, he first has to take the wheel and drive. Or he talks with professional drivers sufficiently long and unrestrainedly to know what they do, to know what roads are like, and the weather, to know what slippery roads mean and to know the unwritten rules. Of these *matters-yonder* he would not notice a thing if he were to put the driver in front of a keyboard. A phenomenologist does not use these tests, or only as a last resort. He cannot believe that what happens at the keyboard can be applied to reality. So he is little inclined to put his patient in front of a keyboard. He wants to talk to him; he tries to put himself in the situation the patient describes. He wants to compare the patient's impression of this situation with his own impression, and his report is the result of this comparison. In his opinion, psychology, like psychopathology, is a communicative, meditative and descriptive science. The psychologist must be able to talk, to sympathize, to see, to consider and to write.

Let us consider the phenomenologist's answer to the question: what is time? True to his method, he begins with an example, well-known in principle and so formulated that most of us can recognize it from our own experience.

A young man is talking with his parents about his childhood. He says, "I'll always remember Sunday afternoon!" When his parents ask him what he means, he continues, "Sunday afternoon! We never felt so rebellious as when we heard you say, 'Let us go for a walk.' We were dressed up, and then we left, but not before we were warned not to walk in the mud, let alone climb trees or something like that. As a rule, we met other parents on the way, with equally neat and glum-looking children, and you talked to them. I can still show you the spot where we used to stand for hours and were supposed to enjoy ourselves." "How often do you think," his parents ask, "we went for a walk like that?" "Oh well, I cannot say exactly, of

78

course," the son replies, "but I guess it was at least once every fortnight." "Then you are wrong," his parents comment. "Our walks weren't like that at all. But at times we had to go visiting—oftener than once in three months, though. And what you're saying about talking to other people—we very much disliked talking in the street. What we did was exchange a few words and, after a minute or so, go on our way." So far the example.

One can see that one does not have to be a neurotic to mythicize the past, for we can take for granted that everyone makes mistakes like that. The mistake is even the rule. In fact, we could not tell one incident from our childhood without criticism from those who were present at the time. Criticism of the way we stress our story, criticism of the frequency with which we make an incident happen. Our tale is never entirely correct. Sometimes, we ourselves, are the critics of our memory. A person who, after a long absence, returns to the scenes of his childhood is almost certainly surprised: it had looked different when he was a child. More intimate, says the sound person; more wretched, says the neurotic. The houses' proportions, their doors and windows, the wideness and the look of the street, the lights in the evening, the sounds of the morning, the way everything looked in the summer, and in the winter. Everything was different, and with this "different," that cannot be verified, do we live, do we let our future be decided. The young man of our example knows better than to coax along his children on Sundays. His memory, not shared by his parents, decides the way he deals with his children.

The first thing that must be said about the past is that it speaks to us in the present. The past is not primarily significant at the time it was taking place: at that time, it may have had hardly any significance. The past is significant now. The boy spent countless Sunday afternoons in complete freedom: that was the past when it occurred. But that past has no function. It is there, available to other people to be made into their past. The past that is significant is the past *as it appears now*. The past that is significant is a *present past*.

After the war, a woman visited the prison in which she had experienced several frightening weeks during the occupation. What struck her more than anything else was that the prison door appeared so small, smaller than she had expected. "To my mind, it was a door twice as high and twice as wide," she stated. When she was asked how large the door seemed to her now, after her visit, she said, smiling, "Well, it *was* a large door I passed; I still think so." Of course, she knew quite well that the door that closed behind her during the war had had an objective size (that is, valid for everyone) which could be checked. The same size, in fact, as the one that drew her attention on her postwar visit. But it wasn't this size that counted. *In the past, which has a hold on her*, the door remained large: the large door, which shut her off from freedom. It should even be said that, immediately after the war, she had been justified—maybe one would even have thought it her duty—to consider the door large and to remember it as large. The difference between war and peace, between occupation and liberty, had been so real that the prison door, just as any object belonging to this difference, had to appear large. That which touches us shows itself in the appearance of objects. When we were liberated, the bread was whiter than ever: we were even certain that bread had never before been so white, just as certain as, we hope, that it will ever be as white again. The airplanes that carried food and were flying low over the cities were never so heavily loaded, even if it is a fact that they could carry loads three or four times heavier. The past has a task. As long as this task is not fulfilled, the past will—in spite of every control—appear in the sense of the unfulfilled task. The prison door can certainly become· smaller; and not by taking its measure with a tape. The prisoner of those days can relieve the enemy of the odium of hostility. If this happens, the part of the door has finished. The door has then become a normal door again. A door for all.

Similar observations arise about the Sunday afternoons of the first instance. With his recollection, the young man does not prove defectiveness of the human capacity to recall the past. He does not fail, but he shows a meaningful relationship. He shows that his upbringing has not been a sequence of insignificant incidents (it never is). Perhaps he shows through his recollection that he has not completely matured. Possibly by mentioning these recollections to his parents, he wishes to get rid of his immaturity.

He who, after years of absence, visits the scene of his childhood and notices that his memory contains a friendlier and more pleasant picture than the reality he is observing, finds that the past has a value it should retain. He will say: "I'd better not come back here," and he is right: it is good for the past to remain as it is. The neurotic, however, is wrong when he avoids the scenes of his childhood. He is trying to escape from a past of a damaging nature. It is, perhaps, time for him to see his past in another light. He may do well by finding a therapist with whom he can discuss his past. If such a discussion results in his feeling better, he has made his past more accessible. Then he can visit the scenes of his past for to be cured means to be able to move. Perhaps he will find mysteries in several places, but there are no longer any closed doors.

Let me summarize all this as follows. The past is not possession of a past time. To recollect is not to return to the anchorage of correctly or incorrectly fixed *engrammata*. The past is *what was, as it is appearing now*. What was: indeed, the Sunday afternoons were spent nicely going for a walk. Yet this is no more than a fact, a skeleton of the past. If this skeleton is to live, it will have to acquire flesh and blood. The past that is real, is real now. Its being real *in this way* is not without meaning. The past plays a part; it has to fulfill an actual task for better or for worse. If the past has no task to fulfill, none at all, then it isn't there: then no recollection of this past is possible.

Of this, psychiatric practice offers striking illustrations. Neurotic, but also psychotic, patients can forget significant events. Sometimes extensive periods seem eradicated. That these periods have not disappeared completely becomes apparent when the patient gets better: he begins to speak of matters that did not come to his attention during his illness. The customary explanation is that the patient has been repressing this period. The incident or period is supposed to have sunk into the unconscious and been stored there for the time being. Often these are significant, occasionally even very significant, incidents or periods that have been sunk in this way. But this is the very fact that makes us doubt the correctness of what is implied by the word "repression." How can a patient have no access to a past that is significant? How, furthermore, can something *sink down?* Moreover: *where to?* What is the unconscious? Without complicated hypotheses, everything remains an enigma. *The past does not play a part* is the phenomenologist's explanation that can be made acceptable for every patient whose condition has been disclosed sufficiently. Occasionally, the past does play a part in the sense that *it is not allowed* to play a part. At those times, it cannot play a part because the present does not let it. The present is of another nature, of such a nature that the past would be too much of a disturbing factor.

A similar connection exists with respect to perception. That which is not playing a part is neither seen nor heard, whereas stimuli doubtless continue to flow to the eye and ear. This means that the actual passage of stimuli takes place, the fact of the perception is there, but not the perception itself. Each of us lives in a house that has aspects we have never observed, although stimuli from these aspects no doubt reach our eyes sometimes even thousands of times. Not everything that happens is an experience.[16] This is true for existence as such, and therefore does not need an explanation. That is the way we live. That is the way we live with the objects around us, with the people around us. That is our relationship with our own past. What has no task, has no reality. It is absent; it is only present as a fact or a condition. Life will decide whether this fact, this condition, becomes reality. Life will also decide how the condition becomes reality. Simple recollection is not given to us. Our recollections have a motive. It is this motive that decides the nature of the recollection: nice, delicious, pleasant, disappointing or worrying.

16. E. Straus, *Geschehnis und Erlebnis.* Berlin, 1930.

The motive decides the past; the reader is invited to notice the words, "motive," "past." This means that, whereas until now this discussion was about the past, it naturally arrives at the future. The motive: *the future*. The future decides the past? Let us see whether this is true. To do so, we leave the relationship of present and past and direct our attention toward the significance of the future. What does the word "future" mean? What does psychology generally teach about the future?

The first thing to be said is that psychology has very little to say about the future. Whereas each one *of us thinks far more of things to come than of those that were*, psychology manages to say much about the past and only little about the future. Can the cause of this remarkable fact be traced to this, that (modern) psychology originated partly from the experience of the psychotherapist? The neurotic has much to say about his past and little about the future, although it must be said that recently, judging from the publications, changes have been occurring. The representative books and articles from around the beginning of the century until about thirty years ago do not contain a single statement about the future, except those statements in which the future is rejected. Occasionally, this is done with such emphasis[17] that one wonders who was averse to the future, the patient or his therapist. At first, until the forties, the therapist tried very hard to keep silent about the future (there is no other way to put it); now his objections have largely disappeared. The patient follows this preference: at first he talked and talked about the things that were, and recently he is finding the words to express his future.

17. I am alluding to the rejection of Maeder's prospective interpretation of the dream.

It must be admitted that the patient generally follows the preference of his therapist; otherwise, he would not get well. If the therapist is a follower of Jung, the patient has archetypal dreams; with a follower of Sartre, they are existential. The patient learns to know the preference of his therapist; he gets ill in the latter's preference so that he can get well in this preference. Even the patient suffering from a serious incurable psychiatric disease can, sometimes to a large extent, follow the preference of his physician. Every patient suffers, apart from suffering from his disease as such, from the disease as it exists in the opinion of his physician. He suffers from his physician's point of view, although this is an odd way to put it. He even suffers from the textbook. In fact, this is true for all diseases, the purely physical as well, yet it is particularly true for the psychiatric diseases. This fact had, and still has, consequences for the history of psychiatry. Symptoms come into existence and disappear, according to the psychiatrist's historically changing opinion, although almost always an essential element of the disease remains unaltered. This fluctuating of the symptoms with the theory applied is most apparent in neurosis. The symptoms vary from time to time, from country to country, from psychiatrist to psychiatrist, and from opinion to opinion. So we must assume that the preference for the past was not, in the first place, a preference of the patient, but mainly a preference of the therapist; and the question arises why the therapist had this preference.

The answer is: the therapist felt a preference for the past because his habit was, in general, to think along the lines of evolution. We are still close enough to the time when this was the mode of thought that we can understand it. The first principle of this way of thinking is that which is, *has come into*

85

existence. To understand something, one has to comprehend its origin. Put another way: everything is the outcome of a development. To understand the present, one must investigate the previous condition. That the present could be understood *from the present* is, even to us, not obvious at first. Even more difficult to believe is that the present is made by the future. How can this be explained? The idea that the present is, until now, the last phase of a process of development is much easier to understand.

Yet this idea of the future making the present is obvious in everyday life. When a person goes out, he goes out to do his shopping—a future. Someone at home may have said: "Please go and get me this or that." As long, however, as the instruction is not a clearly defined matter that is to be realized—as his own future—he stays at home. A person driven from his house by a fire is in a hurry to get outside; that is where he is safe. Is there even a single act determined only by the past? The conditions of a decision are given by the past; the act itself originates from the future, from the expectance, the wish, the fear, the desire. This is true for one's entire life. The past provides the conditions for what is going to happen in life, but the acts of life are rooted in the future. This is equally true for a disturbed existence. The past provides the conditions of neurosis; neurosis itself originates from the inaccessible future. The historical situation of the first therapists (related as they were to Darwin, Spencer and Jackson) prevented them from believing in this.

There was yet another reason, besides evolution, although connected with it, for the therapist to concern himself with the past. What was, is fixed. Not only as an incident that has occurred, but also as an impression in the brain, as an *engram*. What is, is not fixed. What is, is being fixed, also as an impression on the brain. What *comes*, is not fixed at all, it is not there, at least not as an impression, not as an *engram*. How, then, can anything originate from it? Nothing only results in nothing. Where there is no memory, no impression on the brain, no *engram*, no matter, there cannot be a beginning of something either, for there is nothing to start from. If the anatomy of the brain is to be our guide, we can see it no other way. There is the brain, we would say. Then, there are yesterday's impressions, there are those from the day before yesterday, there are those from childhood and there is the place today's impressions will be stored. The factors determining the future, even where happiness and disaster are concerned, are decided by the matters already there—by yesterday's impressions, by childhood impressions and by partial impressions of the present. There is nothing else available, so, consequently, there is nothing else to decide future happiness and disaster. The future is an unengraved part of the brain, no impulse could originate from there. The first therapists were victims of this anatomism, just as everyone else was in those days. Even now, we are still victims, more or less, of anatomism. Can the reader really believe that anatomically undetermined parts of the brain exert influence in our behavior? Until recently, almost every textbook on psychology began with a chapter on brain anatomy. First, the substance, then what happens in this substance and finally, the psychic repercussions of these facts—even if this sequence is illusionary. We nevertheless learned to think this way. This is the future: that which results from *engrammata*. An extrapolation.

Yet even a simple comparison results in other conclusions. We all know that a person can give his career another direction. For instance: a letter arrives inviting him to come and talk about another job. Everything changes. As a result of *engrammata*? Or as a result of the letter sent by an unknown person? There are no *engrammata*. Well now, this is what the future is like. It is outside the sphere of one's own person just as much as the letter is, and, consequently, it acts irrespective of *engrammata* and decides the present. The future is a primary factor.

The future, the letter from another person—is there a real difference? The letter summons a future, a future invoked by the writer, by someone else. A future can also be affected by other things: the finding of a treasure, an oil well in one's garden, for instance. Never does the future originate from a purely personal subjectivity. Even the person who is scheming in silence is bound to affect others sooner or later—those others who were finally included in his schemes. Besides, everyone who associates with other people is realizing a future, however insignificant and near it may be; sometimes only the future of an immediate answer. One's future is connected closely with other people (also with other things). Just as closely connected are *engrammata* and being solitary. *Engrammata* are the individual's possession, stored in a closet called a head. This means that anatomism means individualism. In this way, the three *isms*, evolutionism, anatomism and individualism—hang together. By these three *isms*, the doctrines about time have been determined.

What now, without the three *isms*? An example may smooth the way.

Mr. X wakes up in the morning. Before getting up, he spends a few moments thinking about what the day is going to bring. He does not need much time to do this. The previous evening, or perhaps longer ago, he made plans for the day; or circumstances dictated his plans. The past shaped his day. Mr. X enters a day that has received a certain shape. He may be aware that the way he gets out of bed is connected with the shape received by his day. Some days affect him in such a way that he gets out of bed very quickly. Other days seem less inviting, so that it takes longer for one leg to follow the other. And Mr. X even knows days when he turns over and acts as if the day has not begun.

This example, which is so common that we all are familiar with it shows that the future can hardly be a hazy, hovering quantity. The future is real, so real that in the morning Mr. X lets himself be determined completely. This is possible because there is a close connection between present and future. With the aid of our example, this can be put more precisely. The relation of present and future is such that the present envelops the future. For Mr. X, while getting up does not let himself be influenced by what is really going to happen in the course of the day; something like that would indeed be inconceivable. That which is going to happen later, has not arrived, and, as it does not exist, can have no effects. Quite possibly what really happens on that day is not all in accordance with the way Mr. X got up that morning.

The future is what comes, *as it is coming toward us now*, with the stress on *now* and on *coming*. The future is *coming* toward us; it is *Zu-kunft, a-venir*. The words express motion. When we think of the future, time runs to meet us, and we are there already, in the time that is coming toward us. Before Mr. X gets out of bed, the day has arrived; he was in the day before the day began. Before getting out of bed and into his room, he got into the day.

No one goes for a swim in the river (to take another example) if, in another way, he is not in the river already. That one person is already there in an easy way and another in a hesitating way is illustrated when both actually go for a swim. The first person jumps into the water, the second enters the element, which had appeared to him cold and dangerous, very cautiously.

No one travels to another country if he is not in that country already, even when he does not know it. Always, the future has the slightly paradoxical meaning of *meeting oneself*. The traveler is there already; now that he travels through the country by train, he is meeting himself: he is meeting the self that he made go to this country before boarding his train.

With all this, the future does not stay without function. The swimmer who enters the water with an aversion to it will have a historical reason. Earlier experiences, stories he heard about swimming and drowning, result in his being in the water, already, in such a way that he actually enters the water cautiously. *The past is meeting him out of the future.* Also, the example of Mr. X getting up leads to this conclusion. He enters the beginning of a day that was shaped by the past. If no past had shaped his day, he would not have had a reason to get up, and in all probability would, indeed, have stayed in bed. Yet it is equally true that, if his past was not going to meet him in the coming day, this past would not exist. The same relationship can be established in a disturbed existence. Here, the relationship is generally presented more acutely defined, often even unreasonably so. The neurotic who shrinks from a discussion of his problem is putting his earlier experiences into the coming discussion with so much conviction that he decides to cancel his appointment, to find afterward that he is unable to remember what in his past made him do so. Quite possibly, when asked about it, he does not know anything about his past. Envisaging the future (the discussion), he cancelled his past. Many years can disappear this way, which means *that a future is not possible.* The years return as soon as the future, from out of which these years have to make their appearance, has become accessible.

The result of this short analysis can be summarized as follows. Past and future are not two distinctive spheres touching one another in a zero point called "present." Indeed, past and present differ: the past is there, behind us; the future yonder, before us. Yet both have an actual value; future and past are embodied in a present. The present has dimensions; at times it contains a whole life—as an exception, it may even contain a period longer than an individual existence. The past is within this present: what was is the *way* it is appearing now. *The future*: what comes, the *way* it is meeting us now.[18] This appearing and meeting are closely connected. The past appears in what is coming to meet us; if it does not appear, it is absent. So that, indeed, the past is that which lies there behind us, but only because a future permits it to lie there. And the future is indeed yonder, before us, but only because it is fed by a past. The present is an invitation from out of the future to

18. Compare, for this expression, M. Heidegger, *Sein und Zeit.* Halle, 1927.

gain mastery over bygone times. Now it becomes clear why the neurotic (and often the psychotic) worries about his past, the past that seems chaos to him. *The future became inaccessible,* for an accessible future means a well-ordered past.

Let me clarify the "explanation without the three *isms*" by citing another example.

In a factory, a workman falls from a ladder and breaks his leg. He is taken to a hospital, where the fracture is treated, and after a while the workman, still limping, is permitted to go home. A few weeks later, he is told that the fracture has healed, and he goes back to work. The same day, he finds that his leg still hurts. He consults the factory physician and is advised to work half time for another week. But even this is impossible. The workman stays home, gets in trouble with his benevolence fund and is eventually referred to the hospital for a thorough checkup. Neither the examination nor the X-ray photograph reveals any defects. The patient is told that everything is all right and there is no reason why he should not resume work. The patient is not convinced. He says that he is unable to work. He stays at home, limps and airs his complaints to anyone who is willing to listen to him. What has happened?

An exploration of the patient's life history reveals that there had been conflicts before the accident. He had been unsatisfied with his work, there were tensions between him and his employer and he had been unhappy about his life in general. These aspects are not unrelated. What the connection is, for this patient, is of no significance here. What is significant is the fact that, before his accident, the patient had been in trouble and his difficulties had been connected with his relations with other people—his employer, his colleagues, the members of his family, almost everyone. When he fell, he fell out of his difficulties. Certainly, he broke his leg, and it did hurt. He groaned and sighed, which does not alter the fact that, at the same time, inaudibly, he heaved a sigh of relief. In the hospital, the factory was far away, his family was far away; the patient was fairly well off in the hospital. No sooner did the patient get better than his difficulties returned. Is it so strange that his condition improved so slowly and that he kept complaining?

A slight pain means a clearly notable pain to him; not to walk easily means to limp. Almost everyone has had similar experiences. If we get up in the morning with a slight headache, we generally notice this headache more acutely when the day is not very promising than when the day is filled with pleasant prospects. It would not be right to assume that we are making an exhibition of ourselves in the first instance and making light of the pain in the latter. There is no pain without anything to it. Pain has a meaning; usually the meaning is in harmony with our whole life. This does not mean that the happy person knows no pain. But it does mean that he bears his pain in another way.

What happened to the workman can be summarized as follows: When he found himself in bed in the hospital, he realized that his past had been augmented by a significant incident: the fall and the fracture. The weeks of idleness awaiting him had been determined by this accident. But how? The patient had a choice. How would he bring his accident to his future? In what shape? In the shape which makes his future most accessible. Which, for him (with his difficulties—and his personality!) means the shape of a significant fact: of much pain and much trouble walking. We could say that the patient made no happy choice. An existence with pain and lameness (for the pain and lameness are not simulated, the patient does suffer) is not attractive to anyone. But his existence before the accident knew of another pain and another lameness: the pain of a constant humiliation and the lameness of an enslaved life. This pain and lameness were harder to bear. So the workman made the right choice. Or rather, from a shortsighted point of view, he made the right choice, for had it not been a likely solution for him to solve the conflicts in his work and, if necessary, find another job? He could even get a divorce and remarry; he could make all new relationships for that matter. All this, however, is easy to say. The workman was a difficult person. Who knows how hard it would have been for him to change his job? He was almost compelled to find the kind of disturbance in his fracture that would keep him out of his conflicts. *Compelled to find*: he was, not entirely, *compelled* to make a, not entirely, free choice.[19]

Let us review the whole situation. In the factory (we shall not consider the other conflicts), the workman worked in an atmosphere of conflict. If we should establish that conditions in the factory were indeed difficult, we are still justified in assuming that the patient did not react to these conditions in a favorable manner. Other people managed to carry on under the same conditions. If the relation between man and human environment is compared with a dialogue, the dialogue between this workman and his environment became a dispute— even if there were no harsh words; in all probability, far too

19. Compare, for this definition, J.-P. Sartre, *L'être et le néant*. Paris, 1943.

few harsh words were spoken. The trauma, the fracture, received its significance from this dispute: it was a serious trauma, a very serious trauma, the pain was severe, the victim's face had borne a real expression of pain; his helplessness had been obvious to everyone. The trauma had to play a part, as everything has to play a part in human existence. The part this trauma played was elimination of a conflicting relationship. The trauma had to keep the workman far from the factory, far from the conflicting association which had taken the place of his work, with the result that the patient did not get better. Medically speaking, his leg may have healed, but as long as the conflicting relationship threatened, his leg had to play its part, and because the conflicting relationship was not solved, the pain and the lameness stayed. The patient's recovery must not be sought in the healing of the fracture but in the healing of the conflicting relationship between him and the factory, for this relationship carries the trauma. The relationship makes the trauma serious, and it makes it remain serious.

I should like to discuss the words, "this relationship carries the trauma." When a record of a life history or a psychotherapeutic treatment shows that the father plays a significant and unfavorable part in the life of a neurotic, then, for the time being, we are still not justified in assuming that this particular father, by an objectively bad upbringing, is or was standing in the way of his child's favorable development. A carefully recorded history from other sources may well show that the father did not make more mistakes during the rearing of his child than all fathers do; maybe his father had even made a very good job of it. We are equally unjustified in assuming that the mistakes the father did make (every educator makes mistakes) really had such a damaging effect as the patient wants us to believe. Perhaps the mistakes arose from errors, misunderstandings and frustrations inherent to every education. If, induced by the patient's apparent honesty, we are still inclined to doubt the data from other sources, we still must consider the fact that, generally, the patient has brothers or sisters who, with the same father, did not become neurotic. And only infrequently is the patient the eldest or youngest child, the only girl or only boy, so that exceptional behavior of the father can be imputed to the exceptional position of the child in the family. If there is still reason to doubt the data from other sources, we should realize that, of the many children with an indisputably bad upbringing, only a very small percentage ever consults a psychotherapist. Without wishing to minimize the importance of a good or bad upbringing, we must conclude, also on the ground of the many publications devoted to this subject, that there is no reason to give neuroses the stamp of *educational result*. The same, of course, is true for psychoses.

The only conclusion that can be drawn with certainty from the patient's story is that the contact between the patient and his father is seriously disturbed. Of course, the father gave occasion for this; he did make mistakes (as all fathers do). But the son must have reacted in an exceptional way: he made the mistakes serious mistakes, irreparable mistakes. In this way, the dispute between father and son grew, and everything that occurred between them received its significance from this dispute. The disturbed contact determined the seriousness of every incident. In this sense, there were psychotraumata. When the patient says that the father treated him cruelly, he is speaking the truth, even if a witness would have described the incident as a not entirely unnecessary "rap on the fingers." In this context, the rap on the fingers has the significance of a lashing or a sound whacking. The disturbed contact makes the rap a damaging act. In this way, a smile becomes a sneer, a trivial remark a harsh reproach. The context causes the psychotrauma (although the conditions are never absent).

In other words, the son determines the nature of the rap on the fingers; he does so at the moment of the incident, he does so again later—perhaps much later—and, perhaps, every time in a different way. He determines (with little freedom) the manner in which his father looks at him; he determines how his father speaks to him; he gives significance to everything that takes place between him and his father. When the contact between them is disturbed, then he is compelled to determine the significance of the incident unfavorably. If contact was right, the incidents have a positive significance. It is not necessary for the incidents to assume their significance at the time of their occurrence. Generally, the incident becomes most significant during the period of maturaton. If the maturation fails, which means that the relation between father and son which should be brought to a successful conclusion during the period of puberty, has come to a deadlock, this failure changes all incidents that ever took place between father and son. Everyone knows similar changes from his own experience, for this attitude is not a specifically neurotic one (if it exists at all). A person who gets into difficulties with a former friend and no longer trusts him is inclined to give another interpretation to incidents of the past. The incidents, he finds, are showing themselves in a new light. So is the enamored person inclined to interpret much of what happened between him and his girl before they fell in love, in favor of his love. He tries to equalize the past with the present of his love; he discovers indications of affection in a period in which there was no mention of affection and in which, therefore, all indications were absent, objectively (which means: to all).

In these cases, Dupré spoke of a mythicizing of the past. It could be called delusive recollection or memory falsification. But these and similar words do not give a right impression of what is taking place. The disturbed contact between father and son is no myth; it is reality. This contact is as real as the undisturbed contact between fathers and sons. Then the change in the nature of the incidents of the past may not be called a mythicizing of these incidents. This change is a change into a new reality, into that reality that is necessary in this contact. Once again: the patient is not deceiving himself when he speaks of a psychotrauma; he is telling the truth when he relates his past with his father. Words like "myth" and "delusive recollections" presuppose a past of only one shape, the shape observed by the unemotional, unprejudiced witness at the time of an incident's occurrence. But this unprejudiced past does not exist.

The treatment of the patient, consequently, does not consist of a liberation from his childhood's psychotraumata, but of a liberation from the significance of these psychotraumata through the liberation from the disturbed contact with—in this instance—his father. During the treatment, the patient learns to see his past differently. In the psychotherapist's office, talking, he recapitulates his childhood, his whole life, and while doing this, he realizes that his life could have been different and, consequently, that it can still become different, become better. The patient changes his past, and in so doing, gives his future (from which his past presents itself to him) a new countenance. Obviously, the patient confronts his psychotherapist with the same unfavorable conditions with which he confronted his father. He needs someone in place of his father whom we can come to terms with his father. Yet, in the eyes of an unprejudiced witness, he has no real cause, no actual reason, deductible from the therapist's characteristics, for these unfavorable conditions. Just as little cause, in fact, as can be deducted from his father's characteristics. The father gave cause to these conditions; as an educator, he had a task to fulfill, and anyone with a task makes mistakes. The psychotherapist also has a task, so he also makes mistakes. The words he speaks will be misunderstood by the patient for the same reason that have led the patient to form a low opinion of his father. The patient makes the mistakes of the psychotherapeutic contact—real *mistakes*. But with this difference: in the patient's relations with his father, the therapist, with a methodical routine, extricates him from the peculiarities of his behavior. The patient is confronted with his contact disturbance. The patient does not transfer an affect from his father to the psychotherapist; that really is impossible. The neurotic relationship with his father and the neurotic relationship with the psychotherapist have an aspect in common, his contact disturbance in general. That he is on bad terms with his father is a bad effect of this general contact disturbance; the same contact disturbance brings him into difficulties in the contact with the psychotherapist.

One may be inclined to observe that, in this reasoning, the

99

patient is assigned a great responsibility. Yet what else does the therapist do when he agrees to treat a patient? Nothing can be done about the past as it really happened. The past is over and done with, and besides, the patient is an adult. His father and all the people of the days of his childhood have played their parts. And even if, for a moment, one could accept the possibility of changing the conditions of the patient's childhood, hardly anyone would wish to make any changes. No one would find factors to which one could ascribe a neurosis. Once again: no laurels can be reaped from the past *as it really was*. Yet this means that the therapist who proposes a treatment, in the course of a conversation, tells his patient to what extent he must promote his own recovery. The patient is the one who carries the burden of his past. The psychotherapist is the person under whose guidance the recovery progresses; he knows the method—which the patient accepts. Thus, in this manner the patient is responsible. Does this mean that he must be considered guilty of his neurosis? Doubtlessly, no. Does it mean that the therapist is passive in the process of the recovery? No more than the patient is guilty. The patient was caught in an impasse, without any guilt, often only because of his nature (which does not exclude a recovery from his neurotic condition). He is trying to find his cure in his own existence. In this cure, he alters the roles of the people of his childhood. The therapist plays a part in the cure. Disease and cure are taking place *together with other people*. In the intentionally neutral description of the last words, neither the patient nor anyone else is guilty or responsible. The words "guilt" and "responsibility" are delusive in connection with neurosis and psychotherapy. In general, they are not justified in psychiatry.

It is better not to use these words. They are not needed, either, in the scheme of this chapter, of which the conclusion is: the patient is the owner of his time.

The sound person is more than just the owner. He can do something with his time, without neurotic restraints. In his world, the words "guilt" and "responsibility" are certainly valid. However, guilt and responsibility are words that are mentioned too easily and with too little justification in connection with neuroses.

So far, the conclusions about man and time. The next chapter is devoted to a few particular—so far, hardly mentioned—subjects that are immediately related to the complaints of our patient and which, moreover, should not be omitted in a brief psychopathology.

CHAPTER THREE

Psychopathology: Science of Loneliness

At the beginning of this book the patient's complaints were brought together in terms of categories, while at the same time, I tried not to harm the story itself. There were four categories: complaints about objects, that is, about the material surroundings of the world, as defined in phenomenological publications; complaints about the body; complaints about relations with others; and complaints about the past and the future, the complaints about time. For each of these categories, there seemed to exist a word to elucidate these complaints: projection, conversion, transference and memory distortion, the latter of which can also be defined as misrepresentation of what one can recollect. These four terms are distinct and practical, and insofar as their theory is concerned, they comply with the philosophical belief that man's existence is the existence of a subject with no history, living out his existence in an alien body, which in its turn is being surrounded by strange objects, in the middle of which objects other subjects can be encountered, equally enclosed in alien bodies, equally lacking a history.

If this imagery corresponds but little with our picture of existence as we know it, one must also say that the theory behind the four terms has a rather obscure character. One wonders how a subject can detach something from himself, cast this immaterial something away from himself and finally attach it to matter. Equally unintelligible is that a subject should animate a body, that it should change other subjects and that it should distort its past.

Furthermore, it is remarkable how much these terms imply a negation. Projection denies the patient's observations. Conversion denies the existence of the patient's bodily sensations. Transference denies what the patient can find in others. Memory distortion denies what the patient remembers. The theory is really a fourfold denial of the truth of the patient's reality, and the patient is left with no other alternative than to live within the boundaries of a domain called the subject, which domain appears to have so many restrictions that in the end no one knows what it actually contains.

Finally, one more objection. With the use of these four terms, the distinction between healthy and mentally ill persons is entirely lost. For, if we want to continue using these four terms, then we are correct in saying that every single human being, including the very healthy one, projects, converts, transfers and distorts his memories; for no human being lives in the midst of nameless objects, with a body that is anonymous, surrounded by puppets and equipped with a past that is recorded in *engrammata* and that has no history. On the contrary, everyone lives an existence that is structured, incarnate, interpersonal and historical. This is how it is and not otherwise. In pathology, order, incarnation, interpersonal relations and history all have different interpretations, even though each particular form can help throw light on every other form. All mentally ill people are also human beings. The only difference which using these four words, that would remain between the healthy and the sick person is that projections, conversions, transferences and memory distortions are not conspicuous in the healthy person but are very much so in the mentally ill. The reason for this is that the healthy person will discover in his healthy fellowmen the selfsame, or more or less the same, conversions, projections, transferences and distortions of memory as he himself has, whereas the mentally ill person is alone with his mental mechanisms.

This last finding has always been considered as preeminently important by phenomenologists. The psychiatric patient is alone. He has few relationships or perhaps no relationships at all. He lives in isolation. He feels lonely. He may dread an interview with another person. At times, a conversation with him is impossible. He is somewhat strange; sometimes he is enigmatic and he may, on rare occasions, be even unfathomable. The variations are endless, but the essence is always the same. The psychiatric patient stands apart from the rest of the world. This is why he has a world of his own: in his world, houses can sway forward, flowers can look dull and colorless. This is why he also has a special sort of body: his heart aches, his legs are weak and powerless. His past, too, is different. His rearing has failed, and this in turn causes his difficulties with other people—difficulties that summarize, as it were, all his other complaints. He is alone. He is a lonely man. Loneliness is the central core of his illness, no matter what his illness may be. Thus, loneliness is the nucleus of psychiatry. If loneliness did not exist, we could reasonably assume that psychiatric illnesses could not occur either, with the exception of the few disturbances caused by anatomical or physiological disorders of the brain. We have no knowledge of animals ever having "genuine" mental disorders.

Some psychiatric patients live such an isolated life that a normal person can scarcely penetrate it. This is particularly true of schizophrenics and even more so of all patients whose mental illness is characterized by hallucinations and delusions. So let us consider these two symptoms, which have exerted such powerful influence over psychiatric literature and which have given rise to such deep-going theoretical controversies. First, let us take hallucination.

The oldest known definition[20] of hallucination is as follows: a hallucination is the perception of an external object not really present. The patient hears voices, he listens attentively to what he can hear, but the healthy person standing next to him hears nothing. The patient perceives soldiers in the landscape, he closely watches their movements, but the healthy person standing by can see nothing. The patient can see, hear, perceive, but no object is present. Yet this definition is not quite correct, because the object, which according to this definition is not present, is not present to the healthy person. To the mentally sick patient, it is present. This becomes obvious when one observes him and the way he sees and hears. What is more, and this is our second criticism, the mentally sick man does not really perceive. He hallucinates, and that is not the same thing. For the mental patient can distinguish between his perceptions and his hallucinations just as he can distinguish between both perception and hallucination and perceptual phenomena provoked by artificial stimulation of the brain.

20. By J. E. D. Esquirol, *Des maladies mentales*. Paris, 1838.

The definition, perception without an object being present, really confuses two realities, the reality of the healthy human being and that of the mentally sick patient.

Can we find a better definition? Let us, first, point out that the two shortcomings of this old and often repeated definition are closely connected. The mentally ill patient who has a hallucination does not perceive—this is the first defect; and he has an object that does not exist for us—the second defect. In other words, his hallucination implies having an object that does not exist for us. This definition is an improvement on the first one, but it still remains slightly opaque. The sick person who hallucinates has some objects for himself alone. He has a world of his own that is founded in his isolation. He who is thus isolated has objects of his own. Even the healthy individual subjected to complete isolation hallucinates after a short while. Sooner or later, the lonely person will create his own objects. But do these objects exist at all? Here, again, we have a rather ambiguous question, because once more, two worlds are being confused. The objects most definitely are real and are taken very seriously by the patient (and by the isolated healthy person). In a way, they exist even more for him than everyday objects exist for the not lonely. As it is, the mentally ill (as well as the isolated normal person) takes these objects very seriously indeed. They determine his life, he follows their command and tries to escape from their images. We should not use the word "image" in this context, because what the patient perceives are not images, but objects, people, realities. Should we happen to be isolated, we too would soon perceive probably not the same but similarly real objects. We certainly would also believe in these objects. However, one

107

would then trust our words, and what is more, one could understand us. We would be alone. To try to comprehend the object of a hallucination means to wish that hallucination would equal perception, which in its turn means to wish that the mentally ill would stop being ill. The mentally sick person, once he is better, can tell us nothing sensible about his hallucinations. His hallucinations, his unapproachability and the fact that he cannot be understood are all one and the same thing: his illness. His illness, which consequently leads to total isolation.

The same is true for delusions. The disorder that the hallucinating patient shows in the sphere of perception, dominates the field of interpersonal relationships in the case of a patient suffering from delusions. He thinks, for instance, that a conspiracy has been set up against him. The healthy person notices nothing of this conspiracy, and he cannot prove to the sick person that he is mistaken. The mentally ill is unaffected by the evidence, no matter how convincing it may be and no matter how much it conforms to reality. One even gets the impression that the mentally ill wards off such evidence. The mentally ill will not accept the reality of the healthy. His own reality is different. The mentally ill is alone to such an extent and in such a pathological way that he keeps to his own personal relationships. But can we call them relationships at all? We have here the same question as before and the same answer must be given. The way he relates to the conspiracy is real to him but not to us. With this statement, we have arrived again at the focal point of his disorder. The mentally sick person is alone; he communicates alone, and a healthy person cannot penetrate his world. We are unable to understand the way in which he relates to things. If we could fathom his contacts (the way it is possible to understand the daydream relations of the neurotic), then the patient would not be ill in this particular way. He is ill and alone in such a way that he is living a life filled with relusive relationships.

There is a theory that tries to explain the origin of hallucinations and delusions by a too tenuous, too fragile and too distant link between patient and reality. Hallucination, according to this theory, is supposed to proliferate as a weed on a tract of barren land, which land lies between the person and the surrounding world. To a certain extent, this theory is correct: hallucination and delusion can, indeed, only come into existence when there is a distance between the person and his environment. The one thing that I should like to note is that one should not conceive of the distance between the person and his environment as a condition, in the sense that hallucination and delusion would only be the consequences of this particular condition and not the condition itself. With alienation, isolation, loneliness and other terms along this dismal line, as well as with the word "distance" (the word used by the patient of this book) we can summarize the fact that all these mental states never stand by themselves and are never abstractions, but they ceaselessly reveal themselves in the reality of the surrounding world, in the reality of the objects, in the reality of personal relationships and in the reality of body and of time. Everything is mutually dependent and nothing comes first. No matter at what corner we start first (this imagery is borrowed from Binswanger) we always lift the whole carpet. Therefore, in principle, it is unimportant where we start with the description of the pathological. We can start by specifying

109

the objects, the body, the human relationships or time. Even
if we think that we are adhering to our own particular theme
—the description invariably results in the description of the
whole—everything is connected with everything else.

It is nevertheless true that relationships with others is of
such vital significance in this context that psychopathology
could be called the science of loneliness and isolation, where
the first word is to indicate that the patient himself can really
suffer from his condition and the second word is to denote
that he does not always suffer. The patient of this book did
suffer from loneliness. The schizophrenic patient, on the other
hand, is often so much alienated from sanity that he can no
longer make a distinction between what is well and what is
sick and consequently no longer suffers from his mental state,
his isolation. Between these two poles, a number of forms
and degrees, of course, can be approached through the defi-
nitions of the neurotic and the schizophrenic. Neurosis and
schizophrenia are, indeed, the two opposite points in psychopathology. Insight into these two mental disorders rules the
whole field.

Psychopathology: science of loneliness and of isolation. In-
trinsically connected with loneliness and isolation is one very
important theme of this science, a theme that the reader perhaps would have liked to have had elucidated more fully
earlier in this book and which has so far not come up for discussion—the theme of the unconscious. Considering that this
subject is often confused with one closely related but yet dis-
tinguishable subject, self-concealment, and as the latter lends
itself well for a preamble, I shall start with self-concealment.

In relations with others, one can hide, keep something secret, disguise. One person can lead another astray, deceive him, cheat him. To be brief, one can, as it were, conceal oneself in a relationship. What is the phenomenological meaning of all this? The question is of considerable interest, because phenomenology, with its emphasis on man's revelation by objects, gives the impression of leaving no room for a personal, concealed, even deliberately concealed existence. Let us start the discussion by using the already mentioned example of the keyhole. The reader will remember the passage which I borrowed from Sartre. Here is a man who is peeping through a keyhole. He is bent forward, he is looking furtively at things not meant for his eyes. He is alone, believes himself unobserved and completely loses himself in what he sees. This last statement can be taken all but literally. This man is not where he has actually been standing but has disappeared through the keyhole. That is, at least, what he himself experiences. For the spectator who (let us assume) is secretly watching, there is a man stooping before a door—even though the spectator, too, realizes that the man is completely absorbed by what he observes beyond. No one could possibly stay that long in a stooping position unless one is willing to abandon one's body. That is exactly what this man did: he abandoned his body and disappeared into the room beyond, where there was so much to be seen.

His situation is, however, quite critical. He may be observed, and we suppose he is being observed. As soon as he notices the one who observes him (there may be a noise to warn him), he feels completely defenseless. The spectator can see his body, which he had abandoned and which he, owing to the disapproval the spectator is likely to express, is now incapable of

retrieving. How is he to get his body back? He has to abandon
the room, but that is not sufficient. He has to fight the spectator, he has to undo the spectator's power over his body. One
way to achieve this would be to look at the spectator the way
we do in a railway carriage when we are being stared at—to
banish the spectator from his own field of vision. But most
probably he is at a loss as to what to do in such a situation and
tries to conceal himself. He may say, for example, that suspi-
cious sounds were issuing from the room beyond, so that he
had to peep through the keyhole. As soon as he utters these
words, he conjures up a room that does not really exist for
him but in which he asks the other person to believe. He may
even succeed in placing that room there with such firm conviction that he can enter into details when describing it. His
detailed account of the room may be so plausible that the
spectator actually accepts his words as true. With an example
like this, one can demonstrate the phenomenological meaning
of the word "self-concealment." At the moment of discovery,
the peeping Tom is nowhere. The room has been taken from
him, the room has, as it were, streamed to the other person;
equally plastic is the peeper's body. Sartre says that his body
"clots under the other person's stare." That is to say, the spectator now has the peeper in his power; his very movements
are under his control. The peeping Tom straightens up laboriously, his bodily acts are constrained. The body is no longer
his own but has been taken over by the spectator. Where is
peeping Tom then? Well, we could say that he still is, to some
extent and in a negative sense, in the room and, to some extent
and in a negative sense, in his own body. He is in a state of
absence, he is liable to faint and may even do so. But he does

not faint. He recovers, he unbends, he looks at the other person with no trace of embarrassment on his face and he starts on his defense. As we said, he tells his story; that is, he leaves the room to the other person but prescribes himself what the room must look like. If he is not careful, he may even go so far as to accept his own story as true. If he does, he also takes possession of the room, but it is a room with a false aspect. As a rule, a peeping Tom never goes that far. He just quits the room, prescribes the sort of room it has to be and leaves it at that.

He does the same thing with his body, for body and objects are closely related. The peeper leaves his body to the spectator but dictates himself what his body must be like. His eyes, his hands, his limbs, they all reflect the abandoned room.

Another example of self-concealment is the behavior of the workman discussed earlier, only his is a more pathological kind. Recall: the workman falls off a ladder, breaks his leg, stays in bed for some time, is declared to have recovered but keeps on feeling aches and pains and does not return to his work. This undoubtedly appears to be simulation to the outsider and perhaps to the workman himself, but what is so peculiar is that the workman partly or perhaps even entirely believes his own sham story, his own self-deception. We should, therefore, perhaps replace the word "deception" with another. The workman conceals himself so forcefully and with such urgent necessity that he reaches a point of no return. Perhaps a psychotherapist could make the patient return. But this is beside the point. What has happened in fact? The workman's relations at the factory are strained. If asked before the fall about conditions at his factory, he most likely would have painted an altogether dismal picture. In fact, he often complained about his work and, whenever the occasion arose, about the people. There is, however, little chance that he will give the selfsame picture after the fall. In all probability, he prefers not to talk about his work at all. He talks about his body. Before the fall, he talked about the factory and kept silent about his body. After the fall, he talks about his body and never mentions the factory.

What does this reversal mean? First, the factory. He had expressed dissatisfaction with the factory, and now he does not say a word about it. If one asks him about his working conditions, he will give, in comparison to his former grievances, a fairly dull account of his work. He commits the factory to others. Second, his body. Before the fall, he kept silent about his body; now he is tireless in talking about it. In fact, he complains about a body that happens to be sound. But this body which could be healthy must not be so as far as others are concerned. He commits this sick body to the others. The outsider (one of the others) says: "This man is a liar, he is a deceitful person." The doctor (also one of the others) declares: "We must be quite sure about what is wrong with him; we must examine him once more." Says his wife and a few more people: "He really is a sick man." The correct explanation, however, is, that he conceals himself. He is attempting to leave the factory and his body to others. This is the phenomenological interpretation. Self-concealment is equal to leaving one's body and the surrounding world to others in a self-chosen manner.

We are dealing only with self-concealment here, but if the patient truly believes his own story and if this belief is so strong that no one can, as it were, call him back (while, at the same time, one is certain of the patient's trustworthiness), then the story may serve as an example of what we call unconscious conceptualization. I am not quite sure whether this term can withstand deeper analysis. No doubt there are other stories that, in reverse, could be illustrations of unconscious conceptualization while in fact we have only to do with self-concealment. I shall give one such example and then end this series of examples with an illustration of genuine unconscious conceptualization.

The example of what seems to belong to the realm of the unconscious but is really only self-concealment, I borrow, with much pleasure, from one of Jung's earliest publications.[21] The case history that Jung presents is not only excellent and classic, but it also demonstrates that Jung knew very well and already at an early date that not all that suggests itself under the term unconscious has the right to bear this term. Jung's publication dates from 1913. He gives us the following case history.

A young lady visits a psychotherapist. Her complaints, which include fits of loss of consciousness, are neurotic. It appears that her ailments originate from one particular point in time, shortly before her visit to the therapist, when one evening, after having visited some friends, she was returning home late at night in the company of others. Quite unexpectedly, they found themselves followed by a fast-rolling carriage drawn by horses. The others all stepped aside but not the young lady. She just stood in the middle of the road, and when

21. C. G. Jung, "Versuch einer Darstellung der psychoanalytischen Theorie," *Jahrbuch für Psychoanalytische und Psychopathologische Forschugen*, V, 1913.

the horses approached, she started to run ahead of them. The coachman cursed and used his whip to try to chase her away; but it was useless, she would not heed his warnings. She kept on running in front of the horses, she raced along the street until (with the horses still at her heels) she got to a bridge, and there her strength gave out. She would have jumped into the river if passers-by had not caught her in time. Her disorders date from this incident. She is suffering from traumatic neurosis.

One is justified in asking why the patient had behaved so strangely. She herself does not know. She is not a person to be easily frightened; her life history gives ample proof of this. Was it perhaps the horses? Following this track, the patient seems to recall that, when she was a little girl of seven, she had a dreadful experience involving horses. She went for a drive in a carriage and the horses bolted. The coachman, who was afraid that the horses would make straight for a precipice, jumped off the carriage and shouted to her to do the same, and she did, whereupon horses and all went over the cliff and disappeared.[22]

The explanation of her traumatic neurosis seems to be as follows. As a seven-year-old child, she was incapable of fully experiencing the terror of this episode—the trauma. The episode lay dormant and was only activated when on that memorable night, she heard the horses galloping close behind. Then, that which for 18 years had been buried in the unconscious became unconscious when, in the presence of the therapist,

22. Jung doubts whether this trauma really took place. This doubt is always justified when a patient suddenly, from out of a void, remembers something (p. 349 of the article mentioned in note 21).

she realized that the fright she was experiencing now at the age of 25, was in fact the fright of an earlier time. At the time of the episode, she did not recall the event of her childhood; the terror alone emerged from the past, and the fear and the possibility of a precipice.

We should like to have a more detailed account of this incident, but already the outline of the story is classic and complete. A trauma in early life, followed by a period with no symptoms; then a negligible trauma, inducing exaggerated reactions and finally the symptoms. But Jung is still bothered about the period between the ages of 7 and 25. Admittedly, the trauma was present in the unconscious all those years, but how is one to suppose that anything that had been lying hidden and sealed for so long could suddenly emerge as a result of an insignificant happening? Could one assume that the formula, "horse now is horse then," broke the seal? Why has nothing happened for 18 years? Jung is still unsatisfied and goes deeply into the problem, centering his thoughts on the onset of the fright. Where was she that night and what exactly happened there? She went to the home of a couple she knew for a farewell party for the wife, who, because of nervous complaints, had to leave town to get treatment elsewhere. Several of the company had just taken the wife to the station and put her on the train when, on the way back, the incident with the horses occurred. Jung can no longer accept the interpretation of the galloping horses. He suspects and eventually detects another linkage, and we can summarize his findings as follows.

The patient knew that, should anything happen to her, she would be taken to the house of her friends. She would then be left alone with the husband. And this is what actually did happen. Overcome by terror, she was taken back to the house of her friends and was left alone with the husband. What ensued was what one would expect to happen between a man and a woman who are fond of each other. They had already kissed passionately on previous occasions, and this fact can also throw some light on the wife's neurotic state. But what about the episode with the horses when she was seven years old? The patient puts the horses on stage in order to conceal herself. Encouraged by the therapist, she produces a worthless piece of reality for the purpose of keeping to herself that other reality. Moreover, she recommends to the therapist another body, a body recoiling in fear from the idea of a precipice, because she wants to keep to herself the body that sinned when she forgot all about her reputation. Deceit, concealment— whichever word we may prefer to use, her story has nothing to do with the unconscious. Jung does not want to have this term used in such and similar contexts. One cannot but agree with him. When an unconscious connection serves as a link with the past, the patient will try to conceal.

Are there, however, no moments in the patient's story which would presume the existence of truly unconscious links? Without any doubt, such moments do exist. To begin with, the patient needs an old past to ward off a painful present. She does not know that she is evading the present. For this not-knowing, this unawareness, the term "unconscious" certainly has validity. Furthermore, she wishes to return to the house of the loved one by way of an accident. This is something she does not know, either. So the word "unconscious" can be valid for this link that exists within the present.

Finally, and this is extremely important to note, the patient is unaware of the meaning of her symptoms. When asked about their cause and meaning (including her fainting), she does not know what to say. But why is that so? There must be a reason or a meaning that, as far as this patient is concerned, bears relation to the impasse in her relationship to the couple, her friends. There must be a connection with her (immature) love which, though returned, will not lead to matrimony. With her feelings of shame. With the scandal she must fear. With the pregnancy she must dread. Perhaps, by fainting, she succeeds in eluding her oppressive misery. Who knows, symbolically she may swoon into the bed of her beloved. There are many more links, causes, meanings one could postulate, and they all have one thing in common: the patient is unaware of any of them. She continued to grope, as in the dark, and her search is indeed blind. Perhaps she does not really grasp the meaning of what is asked of her. Associations that come so easily to the observer meet with no response in her. Why is this? What is the significance of the unconscious?

In answering this question, I return to our patient of this book.

Being a student, the patient is often completely engrossed in his study books. In fact, he is incapable of reading anything else with the same peace of mind and concentration. Newspapers remind him of the things in life that make him feel sick. Novels confront him with the other sex, which he tries to shun. His study books on the other hand, touch neither the domain of day-to-day existence, nor that of love. In the field of his studies, he has the freedom to do as he likes. Yet he is not doing so well. For quite some time, he has not passed an examination. He is, moreover, convinced that under existing circumstances he would be unable to answer a single question. Not only would his nerves fail him, but also, and this is important, he cannot remember anything about his subject. Is he not working hard enough? He most certainly is, even more than most of the other students, but he does not seem to get anywhere. He can read a book as often as three times and open it again the fourth time only to realize that it looks as though he had never seen it before. What he reads just does not penetrate his mind. A sort of barrier prevents access to his mind. But how? The patient does not know the answer. Why doesn't he? Why is it that he does not know anything about the nature of this barrier that prevents his reading from penetrating his mind?

The answer must be found in the reading itself. The patient reads a book, but his reading remains ineffectual. What meaning does a book have for him? It is evident that he handles his books with respect: in his bookcase, they stand in neat rows, and in spite of repeated perusal, they look spotlessly clean and show no dog's-ears; he does not lend books to other people. And yet, there are moments when, in a fit of despair, he tears a book to pieces. Why? The patient does not know. Well, after all, he has to find some outlet for his pent-up emotions. This is hardly an acceptable answer. Why, exactly, does he take them out on a book? Is there some sort of relation between his respect for the book and his inclination to destroy it? Why take vengeance on a book? What is the patient's opinion of the authors of his books? Well, they are all wise men, very learned people, paragons of the virtue of knowledge. He cannot tell you anything about them that may bring discredit on them. But he speaks too well of them. He thinks that they are infallible. He calls them his "authorities."

The last word contains the answer to the previous questions. If a reader of a book considers the writer an authority, then that book cannot be read. The patient refuses to accept this answer. True enough, the answer in this form is not yet correct. What meaning does the word "authority" convey to the patient? (It is always imperative to ask the patient about the specific implications of the words he uses.) The word "authority," to the patient, is a collective word that conveys to him the idea of everything that is adult, active, productive and free. A word that makes one crawl. And this is exactly what the patient does. To open a book is, for him, to mortify his body, to crawl in the presence of a book. Can he possibly read under such circumstances? If so, he still cannot possibly gain knowledge, for he who gains knowledge is a partner—even if at the same time he is only a student. Even he who opens the Bible is a partner. To read, to study, is the same as to participate in a joint enterprise of doing, thinking, considering together. The rebellious slave cannot study. His reading is servile; he will not appropriate any knowledge and will occasionally destroy his books. Here, then, is the answer to the question as to why the patient's reading is so worthless. Because we can equate his reading with rebellion.

Would the patient himself accept this answer with the supporting remarks? Undoubtedly he would not. Why? The answer is clear enough. The question as to the meaning of the unconscious is still open. Why is this patient unwilling to acknowledge his own deeds? Because any admission would clash with his actions. Let us try to put ourselves in the patient's shoes. To him, the writers of books are free, autonomous, dominating figures. This is because all adults around him—including his father—are free autonomous, dominating figures. But the therapist also belongs to this world of free, autonomous, dominating figures. What would it mean if the patient should tell that dominating figure, the therapist, that he could agree with him? It would mean that he would cease regarding the therapist as a dominating person. He would be able to think, judge, decide jointly with the therapist. He would be better. But he is not really better. He cannot share the therapist's insight. He does not understand that the therapist wishes him to get better. The patient's failure to understand the therapist *is* his disorder. His not-knowing means that he is different from other people who do know. The fact that the therapist knows is essentially the same as that the patient is mentally ill and does not know. The consciousness of the therapist is the unconscious of the patient. What, then, is in the patient? Nothing. What we should find in him is awareness with the therapist, the authority. This awareness will come to him when he recovers from his illness. For then the therapist will come near him. Then all mature people will come near him. Then he himself will become mature.

A similar connection can be demonstrated in the case of Jung's patient at the three particular points in her story when the word unconscious is well-grounded. Firstly, she does not know what she evokes in the past in order to camouflage the present. If she knew, she would share the therapist's mentality, freedom, insight and especially his sexual maturity (all qualities which, let us hope rightly, she expects to be present in the therapist). She does not do this because of the nature of her neurosis. Secondly, she does not know that she handles the incident in the street as an instrument to further her own love affair. Once more: if she knew, she would be sexually mature, that is, not ill. Thirdly, she is not aware of the significance of her symptoms. She is mentally ill. If she could interpret the meaning of her symptoms, she would be healthy, just as healthy as the therapist is, who knows about her symptoms. He, the therapist, knows what she does not know. What is unconscious in her is conscious in the therapist.

What we call the unconscious, is it really still unconscious? The term is misleading indeed. It postulates that the content of the unconscious should be found with the patient, while it is exactly this content which the patient lacks—until she gets better. Thus it would be preferable to talk about insight in others. However, the term "unconscious" has become as popular as terms like projection, conversion, transference and memory distortion. There is little prospect that these terms will be discarded very soon.

No, they will stay with us, these popular, much repeated terms. But perhaps we could try to find another interpretation of them. For the theory that underlies these words demands all kinds of concessions, with the final result that the theory fails, and a hypothesis has to be set up to expound a special field of psychic life, called the unconscious, which in its turn has to make up for the deficiencies of the theory. Does phenomenology need this hypothesis? Well, no, it does not require any such hypothesis. The unconscious is knowledge in others, insight which is in others: a characteristic of a special, pathological relation. No "deep layers of the personality" out of which we can explain a number of other obscure phenomena or processes in other not-so-deep layers. For the phenomenologist, there are no layers, there is just one layer (which we must not call a layer at all) of life as such. There, in that life is the

123

depth of life. There is the explanation of life, insofar as life can be explained at all. For there is much that cannot be explained in life and that never has been explained. Life is definitely not a nebula, but it is certainly a mystery. And so it be.

The phenomenologist never needs hypotheses. Hypotheses emerge where the description of reality has been discontinued too soon. Phenomenology is the description of reality. That is why there are so many examples in the book borrowed from life as such: from reality.

Short Discussion of the Literature Concerned

The reader who wants to acquaint himself with the history of phenomenological psychopathology and psychiatry quickly and yet completely and who does not flinch from consulting the sources can be recommended a few publications of Ludwig Binswanger. This Swiss psychiatrist, who must be called the father of phenomenological psychopathology, during his prolific life again and again took up his pen to report in clear words on the state of affairs. His book, *Problem der allgemeinen psychologie* (Berlin, 1922), offers a well-rounded consideration of the new roads psychology could take in the beginning of the twentieth century. The effects of these new options on psychiatry can be found in Binswanger's article, "Ueber Phanomenologie" (which appeared in the *Zeitschrift für die gesammte Neurologie und Psychiatrie of 1923*. This article was also published in the first part of *Ausgewählte Vorträge und Aufsätze* (Bern, 1947).

How extensively general psychology changed in the subsequent period is shown by Binswanger in his great work, *Grundformen und Erkenntnis menschlichen deseins* (Zurich, 1942); the psychiatric consequences of these changes are explained by him in the article, "Ueber die daseinsanalytische

Forschungsrichtung in der Psychiatrie" (*Schweizer Archiv für Psychiatrie und Neurologie*, 1946) and "Daseinsanalytik und Psychiatrie" (*Nervenarzt*, 1951), and in his book *Der Mensch in der Psychiatrie* (Pfullingen, 1957).

These six publications are an excellent introduction to the history of phenomenology and to the application of phenomenology in psychiatry. The following list of works with a short historical commentary may be helpful to the reader who wishes to be informed more extensively.

In 1894, the article, "Ideen über eine beschreibende und zergliedernde Psychologie" (reprinted in the collected works, part IV, Leipzig & Berlin 1924; second print, 1957), appeared from the hand of the well-known philosopher-psychologist, W. Dilthey. It initiated the development of phenomenological psychology. The author analyzes the methods of psychology as exemplified by the works of Wundt; he concludes that these methods have been derived from physical science. Like the physicist, the psychologist tried to dissect the object of his studies; he tried to isolate the elementary factors of mental life to reconstruct actual mental life with these elementary factors. While it was obvious, even then, that the set aim, an all-embracing psychology, could not be achieved in this way, Dilthey was the first to point this out, saying that methods being utilized are not suited to psychology. In his opinion, the essential characteristic of the psychic aspect of human life is that it is a totality, not a collection of elements. Trying to describe an element means leaving the field of psychology. There is no such thing as a psychic element. There is no elementary perception or elementary sensation. The psychologist has to abandon the methods of physical science. He must try to find a method that originates from the subject itself. The psychologist can expect no greater results from the tools of the physicist than a painter can from the tools of a blacksmith. As the subject of psychology, human existence, is always a *totality*, psychology cannot employ a method that dissects wholes into elements. It should be a description of a totality. For the same reason, the aim of psychology can never be explanation. For explaining means building up, and nothing can be built up without elements. The aim of psychology is the rendering of a totality. *Die Natur erklären wir, das Seelenleben verstehen wir*—these words become famous. The aim of psychology is to observe, to comprehend, then to render explicit, to explicate clearly, what was at first seen vaguely in the first comprehension. A person who sees a child cry because it cannot find its toys considers what he is seeing quite comprehensible. If he is a psychologist, he will want to record what seemed comprehensible to him. The physiologist wants to explain: he wants to know the stimulation causing the lachrymal gland to secrete and so on; all of them facts, not very helpful to the psychologist when he tries to elucidate what he has observed comprehensively, perhaps at a glance, perhaps after looking a bit longer, but never by means of the method of the closer investigation.

The distinction Dilthey made between "explaining from elements and "observing comprehensively" had been known for a long time. It had been emphasized by Blaise Pascal (1623-1662). In a manuscript found after his death, *Pensees sur la religion* (1669), he distinguishes the *esprit de géométrie* from the *esprit de finesse,* a distinction similar in many points to the distinction made by Dilthey. It would be interesting to follow up the history of this distinction in attitudes and scientific methods. Then I should mention thinkers like J. G. Herder (1774-1803), Kierkegaard (1813-1855), Nietzsche (1844-1900), Max Scheler (1874-1928), Maine de Biran (1766-1824) and Henri Bergson (1859-1941), authors who all had something to do with the development of phenomenological psychology. But the subjects treated by these authors lead to the field of culture-philosophy, and that is not the intention of this book.

The person who first introduced Dilthey's distinction into psychiatry was Karl Jaspers. In his article, "Kausale und verstandliche Zusammenhange zwischen Schicksal und Psychose bei der Dementia praecox (Schizophrenie)" (*Zeitschrift für die gesammte Neurologie und Psychiatrie*, 1913), he shows that the two methods, when applied to the study of schizophrenia, both lead to satisfactory results, but that only the results of the descriptive method may be called psychological. Jaspers then applies, successfully, the new phenomenological method to the entire field of psychopathology: *Allgemeine Psychopathologie* (Berlin, first print 1913; 338 pages; several reprints), a book, which, irrespective of its phenomenological value, may be considered unrivaled as a survey of psychopathology.

Jaspers' example was followed by many. In numerous publications, new territories were opened by means of the phenomenological method. I shall confine myself to mentioning a few of the most important ones: E. Kretschmer, *Der sensitive Beziehungswahn* (Berlin 1918); K. Birnbaum, *Psychopathologische Dokumente* (Berlin, 1920); and H. C. Rümke, *Zur Phanomenologie und Klinik des Glücksgefühls* (Berlin, 1924).

Briefly put, the procedure that led to such fine results in

these studies comes to this, that an exact and exhaustive description was given of what the psychiatric patient experiences, of what is going on in his mind. It should be noticed that, in the meantime, the phenomenological procedure in this sense of the word, was no longer applied as often as before. It was Binswanger who, in his article, "Ueber Phanomenologie" (*Zeitschrift für die gesammte Neurologie und Psychiatrie*, 1923), made it clear that important fields of psychological and psychopathological activity remained bare if phenomenology was understood to be only exact description of intrapsychical experiences. To illustrate his point, he referred to the work of Edmund Husserl, which was then quite unknown in the psychiatric world, *Logische Untersuchungen* (three parts; Halle, 1900, 1901), in which this philosopher-psychologist extended the important work of his tutor, Franz Brentano ([*Psychologie vom empirischem Standpunkt* (three parts; Leipzig, 1874]). In his book, Husserl makes a distinction which has been exhaustively discussed in the preceding pages, so that I need not go into it here: the distinction between (I did not use these words) "objective" and "categorical." The objective (better, generally valid) perception is the perception of the "closer investigation," the perception of the physicist and the physiologist. The categorical perception, on the other hand, is the perception as it takes place in everyday life. In categorical perception, there is no gap between man and world; the world is human nature's dwelling place, and the dwelling place of nature's peculiarities. The dwelling place, also, of illness. Phenomenology originates from the categorical perception and not, as was advocated by Jaspers, from (precise) introspection. Binswanger's argument comes down to this, that the phenom-

129

enologist should not direct his glance "inwardly" but "outwardly." Expressed paradoxically, true introspection is effected by means of the physical sense of sight; we are seeing ourselves when we observe the world—in which sentence the words "seeing" and "observe" are concerned with categorical, and not objective, perception, a distinction made by neither Dilthey nor Jaspers.

The effect of Binswanger's article is comparable to that of Jaspers' article of 1913. Soon phenomenological publications appeared in which the word "phenomenology" bore the new meaning, *elucidation of prereflective existence.* This has also been discussed in the previous pages. It is important not to confuse these two forms of phenomenology: the Dilthey-Jaspers type and the Husserl-Binswanger type.

The studies signifying the new approach, where the description of sound and disturbed conditions of existence is involved are, among others, L. Binswanger, "Lebensfunction und Lebengeschichte" (*Monatschrift für psychiatrie and Neurologie,* 1928); and E. Straus, *Geschehnis und Erlebnis* (Berlin, 1930).

It is impossible to do more than refer to the works that contain phenomenological investigations into the normal and the disturbed human, space and time. Where *time* is concerned: V. E. von Gebsattel, "Zeitbezogenes Zwangsdenken in der Melancholie" (*Nervenarzt,* 1928); and E. Straus, "Das Zeiterlebnis in der endogenen Depression und in der psychopatischen Verstimmung (*Monatschrift für Psychiatrie und Neurologie,* 1928). Once more, independently of one another, these two psychiatrists then published articles on *space* (as experienced by neurotics with obsessions): V. E. Gebsattel, "Die

Welt des Zwagskranken" (*Monatschrift für Psychiatrie und Neurologie*, 1938). Some time earlier, the latter had published an absorbing article in which he contemplated a general phenomenology of space: E. Straus, "Die Formen des Räumlichen" (*Nervenarzt*, 1930). The theme of this book was later elaborated in a book that may now well be called a standard work: E. Straus, *Vom Sinn der Sinne* (Berlin, 1935; re-edition, 1956). As the title of this book indicates, the author tries to formulate a new psychology of the senses, which, as may be expected, consists of a new psychology of the (perceptible) world.

The author who was the first to apply the Husserl-Binswanger phenomenology to the group of schizophrenic disturbances was F. Fischer. I mention two of his many publications. The first is concerned with the psychopathology of time, and the second has space and the schizophrenic patient for a subject: F. Fischer, "Zeitstrukter und Schizophrenie" (*Zeitschrift für gesammte Neurologie und Psychiatrie*, 1929) and "Ueber die Wandlungen des raumes im Aufbau der Schizophrenen Erlebniswel" (*Nervenarzt*, 1934).

Completely apart, also because of the fact that, for many years, the author worked in Paris, stands the still too little-known book of E. Minkowski, which makes a serious, in many aspects, laudable, effort to comprehend psychopathology from the disturbance of time perception: E. Minkowski, *Le temps vécu* (Paris, 1933). Before this, the author had published a work on schizophrenia, which, although not written in a strictly phenomenological tradition, is of an unmistakably phenomenological nature: E. Minkowski, *La Schizophrenie* (Paris, 1927).

In 1933, a book appeared that demonstrated to what extent

the authors of the works mentioned above still failed to draw all the consequences from Husserl's fundamental observations. Again it was Binswanger who removed the remnants of the physicist's way of thinking, so firmly anchored in psychopathology. The result was a completely new pathography, which may be called revolutionary: *Ueber Ideenflucht* (Zurich, 1933; the work first appeared in the form of two articles in *Schweizer Archiv für Psychiatrie und Neurologie*, 1931-32).

This book too, was preceded by a philosophical work, written by a pupil of Husserl, which paved the way to a new, original description of human existence as such. It was M. Heideggerger's *Sein und Zeit* (Halle, 1927), a book that wrought a complete change in the west European world of thought. Binswanger's publication is a direct consequence of this pioneering work.

So three periods can be distinguished in the history of phenomenological psychiatry. The first period was inaugurated by Jaspers (1913), the following two periods by Binswanger (1923, 1933). Each period was preceded by a new reflection on the nature of human existence (by Dilthey, Husserl and Heidegger). However, whereas there is a very clear distinction among the three periods where the term "phenomenology" is concerned, the last two periods merge so harmoniously that the meaning of the word as defined by Husserl need not be changed.

Binswanger's *Ueber Ideenflucht* belongs to the class of rare works that have changed the appearance of psychiatry. It can be put in the category of Esquirol's *Maladies mentales* (1838), the 5th edition of Kraepelin's *Psychiatrie* (1896), Freud's *Traumdeutung* (1900), Bleuler's *Dementia praecox, oder*

Gruppe der Schizophrenien (1911), Bonhoeffer's *Symptomatische Psychosen* (1911), Jaspers' *Psychopathologie* (1913), Kretchmer's *Körperbau und charakter* (1921) and Sullivan's *Conceptions of Modern Psychiatry* (1940).

Ten years later, Binswanger wrote the first comprehensive phenomenological pathography of a patient, suffering from an atypical form of schizophrenia (or, if preferred, suffering from a severe form of schizoid hysteria): "Der Fall Ellen West" (*Schweizer Archiv für Psychiatrie und Neurologie*, 1945), followed soon by three studies also concerning schizophrenia: "Washnsinn als lebensgeschichtliches Phänomen und als Geiteskrankheit" (*Monatschrift für Psychiatrie und Neurologie*, 1945), "Der Fall Jürg Zünd" (*Schweizer Archiv für Psychiatrie und Neurologie*, 1947) and "Der Fall Lola Voss' (*Schweizer Archiv für Psychiatrie und Neurologie*, 1949).

Binswanger's pupil, Roland Kuhn, wrote the first phenenological pathography of a sexually disturbed patient, "Analyse eines Mordversuches eines depressiven Fetischisten und Sodomisten an einer Dirne" (*Monatschrift für Psychiatrie und Neurologie*, 1946); while, in the meantime, the well-known, also Swiss, psychiatrist Medard Boss tried to formulate an entire pathosexuology on the new principles: *Sinn und Gehalt der sexuallen Perversionen* (Bern, 1947).

Häfner was the first to write a phenomenology of psychopathy: H. Häfner, *Psychopathen* (Berlin, 1961).

In the Netherlands, van der Horst and his pupils made a serious attempt to describe all psychiatry from new (not only phenomenological) principles: L. van der Horst, *Anthropologischen Psychiatrie* (2 parts; Amsterdam, 1946).

In the field of psychosomatics (if one may use this word in

133

a phenomenological connection without further explanation), Victor von Weizsäcker broke new ground, with his fellow workers and pupils. Von Weizsäcker, who died a few years ago, was head of the internal clinic of Heidelberg University. I will mention two works from his pen: *Studien zur Pathogenese* (Wiesbade, 1935; a concise, clear book almost a statement of principles, written in such a way that it is accessible to the layman) and the considerably larger work, *Fälle und Probleme, Anthropologische Vorlesungen in der Medizinischer Klinik* (Stuttgart, 1947).

This work, *Fälle und Probleme*, which consists of sixty lectures, is one of the finest studies in the field of phenomenological pathology. Because this work is also of a simple nature, so that it provides no difficulties to students who are not conversant with this subject matter, I can recommend it as an uncomplicated, yet profound general introduction to the field of phenomenology. The patients discussed in this book are nearly all patients with internal defects. This makes the book of exceptional importance also to the general practitioner and the specialist-somatologist.

Numerous publications appeared from von Weizsäcker's clinic. I will only mention H. Heubschmann, *Psyche und Tuberculose* (Stuttgart, 1952).

Works like these raise the question as to the nature of the method used in somatic medicine. The reader who wants a clear phenomenological answer is recommended by W. Metz's paper" *Het verschijnsel pijn. Methode en mensbeeld der gneeskunde.* (Haarlem, 1964).

A few words about the changes that took place in France. A philosophical work, significant in connection with the matter treated here, that met with a widespread general response also appeared in this country: J. P. Sartre, *L'être et le néant* (Paris, 1943). Husserl's and Heidegger's influence can readily be detected in this work. The book offers excellent examples of phenomenological insight. Particularly the chapters on the human glance and on the body may be judged among the best ever written on a phenomenological subject. Strangely enough, this work, until the present, exerted hardly any influence on French psychiatry (which was, again, clearly illustrated by the beautifully written, well-arranged, but, in a sense, almost helpless work of G. Lanterni-Laura, *La psychiatrie phénomenologique* [Paris, 1963]). This is the stranger, because French psychology was strongly influenced by it. Although their studies fall outside the scope of this book, I cannot refrain from mentioning a few French psychologists whose works are colored by Sartre's philosophy: Merlau-Ponty, Jeanson, Mounier and, to a lesser degree, Georges Gusdorf. The latter's book, *La découverte de soi* (Paris, 1948), is of invaluable significance to a new (phenomenological) psychology.

The work of Gaston Bachelard deserves special mention. Not noticeably influenced by the new trends in the German and French philosophy, he designed a psychology of the elements of fire, water, air and earth, as can only be written by a phenomenologist. His publications seem to me of immediate value to psychopathology. Of these publications, I mention the following: *La psychanalyse du feu* (Paris), *L'eau et les rêves* (Paris, 1942), *L'air et les songes* (Paris, 1943), *La terre et les rêveries de la volonté* (Paris, 1948) and then the work which summarizes his views, *La poétique de l'espace* (Paris, 1951).

A Different Existence

Now that, with the last-mentioned authors, I find myself in the field of phenomenological psychology. I shall mention two more authors who showed that phenomenology leads to exceptional results in psychology: O. F. Bollnow, whose book on the moods appeared in 1943, *Das Wesen der Stimmungen* (Frankfort), and the Dutch psychologist F. J. J. Buytendijk, who, by his personal leadership and by a list of excellent works, rendered such exceptional service to Dutch psychology.

The French psychotherapist R. Desoille may be considered one of the designers of a very individual and original mention: *Le rêve éveillé en psychothérapie* (Paris, 1945) and *Psycho-analyse et rêve éveillé dirigé* (Bar-le-Duc, 1947), which two studies (although the author was unaware of it) lean on a therapeutic principal of Binswanger, that is, that the (day) dream is not only a result of an unsatisfied desire but must also be considered a trial act, and thus an auto-therapeutic act.

The reader can find Binswanger's views on this subject (which are certainly influenced by the investigations of his fellow countryman A. Maeder) in *Traum and Existenz* (Neue Schweizer Rundschau, 1930), which was reprinted in Binswanger's *Ausgewählte Vorträge und Aufsätze* (T. I. Bern, 1960).

A comprehensive phenomenology of the dream and dream interpretation has been given by the already mentioned author Medard Boss in his hardly enough praised *Der Traum und seine Auslegung* (Bern, 1953).

A pupil of Boss wrote a first general phenomenological psychotherapy, G. Condrau, *Daseinsanalytstische Psychotherapie* (Bern, 1963), in which title appears (not for the first time in my summary) the word *Daseins-analyse*. The word *Dasein*, in the much-implying sense of "to be there" or "to be with the objects," has been derived from Heidegger. The word *Daseins-analyse* was coined by Binswanger and means analysis, by means of *description*, of the existence of the sound, and of the disturbed, person, as an existence that realizes itself *there*. My list is far from being complete. Particularly the Dutchmen, who have been so active in the field of phenomenology, have not been mentioned often enough. Without referring each time to the publications (the reader can find them easily enough) I shall mention the names of the psychologists and the psychiatrists in the Netherlands who have played a part in the development of phenomenology. The psychologists, beside Buytendijk whom I mentioned, are M. J. Langeveld, D. J. van Lennep and J. Linschoten. The psychiatrists (among whom I mentioned Rümke and Van der Horst) are P. Th. Hugenholz, A. Hutter, A. J. Janse de Jong, E. Verbeek and E. L. K. Zeldenrust. I do wish to mention a study by the last-mentioned author, certainly belonging—as the only phenomenologically minded monograph on hysteria—to the field covered in this book: E. L. K. Zeldenrust, *Over het wezen der hysterie* (Utrecht, 1954).

The reader who wishes to read a more or less complete summary of foreign authors, furnished with a good commentary, may be referred to Herbert Spiegelberg, *The Phenomenological Movement* (two parts; The Hague, 1960). That this work appeared in English must be considered of exceptional importance. It provides the American reader (the British have, until now, shown little interest in phenomenology) with the means to be informed quickly and well about all that has happened in this field in Europe, now that, in America itself, there

137

is a growing interest in phenomenology. The American phenomenology is definitely of a nature different from that of the European—less philosophically concerned, more sociopsychological in its applications. The reader who wishes to be informed about the phenomenological state of affairs in the United States is recommended, first of all, a work that seems to have hardly anything to do with phenomenology: G. H. Mead, *Mind, Self and Society* (Chicago, 1934), a study which, in several places, reveals a phenomenological way of thinking. After this, the reader may read a few of the works of Karen Horney, which are no more connected with what is officially called phenomenology, for instance, her *New Ways in Psychoanalysis* (London, 1939), in order, after this introduction, to find his way to the very original American psychiatrist: H. S. Sullivan, *Conceptions of Modern Psychiatry* (New York, 1940).

To show that there is a growing interest in the United States for phenomenological (or existential) psychiatry and psychotherapy, I mention three periodicals: *The Journal of Existential Psychiatry* (first year of publication, 1960), the *Review of Existential Psychology and Psychiatry* (first year of publication, 1961), initially edited by A. van Kaam, and the *Journal of Phenomenological Psychology* (first year of publication, 1970) published by Duquesne University Press, to which can be added a fourth, which is not directly concerned with phenenological psychology and psychopathology, as such, but which occasionally contains an article on these subjects, *Philosophy and Phenomenological Research* (first year of publication, 1940), edited by Marvin Farber. Finally, where the United States is concerned, a collective work: *The Phenenological Problem*, edited by A. E. Kuenzli (New York, 1959).

I said before that American phenomenology is of a different nature from that of Europe. But now I must name one exception, Duquesne University. There are graduate programs (MA and Ph.D.) in both philosophy and psychology departments that are directly based on the thought of many of the men whom I have just listed. It is a center for the application of phenomenological thought to both clinical and research problems in psychology, as well as a source of a number of publications.

I could leave it at this summary, but for the desire to state, once again, that phenomenological psychology and phenomenological psychopathology both lean on a well-considered and consciously philosophical foundation. Therefore, I give two more works in which this foundation is clearly and ably explained: W. Luypen, *Existentiele fenomenologie* (Utrecht, 1959); and S. Strasser, *Fenomenologie en empirische Menskunde* (Arnhem, 1962). And finally, to terminate my summary, a work which places phenomenology in a general framework of cultural history (in which it belongs), O. F. Bollnow, *Existenzphilosophie* (Stuutgart, 1949).

This is my brief summary of the pertinent literature, which, however carefully composed, is no doubt incomplete because I forgot to mention a few authors. I should like, therefore, to finish this book by offering my apologies to these authors and my thanks to all of them.

Postscript

In 1954, at the request of the late Professor H. J. Pos, I wrote a simple phenomenological psychopathology for the American reader. The booklet was published in 1955, in the *American Lecture Series* by the editor Thomas in Illinois, under the title *The Phenomenological Approach to Psychiatry*. When this book, the Italian translation of which was published in 1961 by Bompiani, Milan (*Fenomenologica e Psichiatria*), was sold out in 1963, the copyright returned to me. After consultation with my editor, I decided to have this study published in Dutch. I read the old text, changed it, and was soon aware that a general revision was necessary. Some passages no longer seemed appropriate, in other places I added a few sentences. The result was an entirely new text, in which, however, the text of the former American edition remained recognizable. As far as I was able, I brought the summary of the literature up to date.

Once more I have reason to be grateful to the editor for his accurate and fine production.